T0064516

His Plans My Hope

Binky Theodore

authorHOUSE®

AuthorHouse™
1663 Liberty Drive
Bloomington, IN 47403
www.authorhouse.com
Phone: 1 (800) 839-8640

© 2015 Sabina Theodore. All rights reserved.

No part of this book may be reproduced, stored in a retrieval system, or transmitted by any means without the written permission of the author.

Published by AuthorHouse 08/10/2015

ISBN: 978-1-5049-2912-7 (sc)
ISBN: 978-1-5049-2911-0 (e)

Print information available on the last page.

Any people depicted in stock imagery provided by Thinkstock are models, and such images are being used for illustrative purposes only.
Certain stock imagery © Thinkstock.

This book is printed on acid-free paper.

Because of the dynamic nature of the Internet, any web addresses or links contained in this book may have changed since publication and may no longer be valid. The views expressed in this work are solely those of the author and do not necessarily reflect the views of the publisher, and the publisher hereby disclaims any responsibility for them.

Contents

For I know well the plans I have in mind for you says the Lord, plans for your welfare and not for woe!

Plans for your future full of hope.

Jeremiah 29:11

Introduction

St. Pope John Paul II, Pope Benedict XVI and Pope Francis have been beckoning a "New Evangelization" in the Church for decades. It is a call for all Christians to humbly and courageously share the *real, personal, and concrete* stories of their otherwise seemingly un-special and un-noteworthy lives. The truths of our Faith do not change, and those truths are easily accessible in Church meeting rooms, in Bible Studies, RCIA Classes, YouTube videos, Catholic blogs, tweets and posts, as well as in a wealth of video series and books created by scholars and theologians of our time. But it's the intimate and personal stories of real people—the "commoners" of society, that best reveal God's masterful love, truth and fidelity in a world desperate for proof that there is somehow purpose to our existence, to our sufferings and to our hope for the future.

This is what motivated me to write my story—the hope that through it someone may come to know and trust God just a little bit more. I am not a celebrity; I have no letters of prestige following my name; I have no degrees in theology, psychology or medicine; and the only people who know me at all are my family and members of my church. But I do have a story. A story of God's perfect, faithful, awe-inspiring, and trustworthy love. May He use it to help you recognize Him in your own story, and help you to persevere, surrender and trust Him in all things.

CHAPTER ONE
Expectations

I was born in 1970 and grew up in suburbia Lancaster, Pennsylvania with my Mom, Dad, sister and two brothers. Lancaster is where both Mom and Dad grew up, and I suppose no reason to leave was ever more captivating than building a life at home.

Though all four of us kids were born within five and a half years, we lived in a neighborhood filled with other kids, and we created closer bonds with them than with each other. We experienced the same love from the same parents and shared the same dining room table for breakfast and dinner, but outside of the shared girls' room and boys' room, most of our time was spent with the kids we went to school with. There were always extra kids in the house and though their parents always referred to my parents as "Mr. and

Mrs. Lefever", all of our friends were introduced to them as "Mom" and "Dad"—and that usually stuck.

As for names, Mom always told me she wanted a little girl named "Binky". She heard it at some point in her life and it had always stuck with her. She knew she couldn't baptize me by that name, so she and Dad gave me my "other" name: Sabina. That was "Sabina Marie" when Mom really wanted to get my attention. I will never forget my very first day of school. When Mom walked me into the classroom, my kindergarten teacher reached for a nametag with a picture of Lucy from the Peanuts' cartoon on it and the name "Sabina" already written on it. Mom looked at my teacher and corrected her by saying, "Her name is Binky. You will call her Binky and you will change her nametag right now before I leave." Obeying my Mom was always highest on my priority list, so I never questioned her about my name and never answered to anything else but "Binky".

Mom always called me her "Little Domesticate". Though I had several friends within a few houses down and across the street, I was most contented to entertain myself. All I wanted to do was play with my baby dolls and Barbie dolls. I was never interested in playing outside or getting my hands dirty. Mom never could quite understand how I always seemed to be the one with the bumps and bruises and trips to the emergency room; but maybe I just didn't mind being the one lifted up to the kitchen counter to get cleaned off, sealed with a band-aid, and healed by Mom's all-powerful kiss.

Once when I was about six years old Mom asked what I wanted to be when I grew up. With all the purity, honesty and sincerity of a child I answered, "I wanta be just like you and do nothing!" Not likely an answer I will ever live down, but it is still true even to this day, now going on forty-five. Mom was a loyal wife, a "stay-at-home mom" and a "homemaker", and I have never wanted to be anything but just like her. She was always there. Always, *always* there. Truly the greatest gift God could ever give me.

Along with being the self-contented, baby-doll-carting, injured child of the family, I was also teased and reprimanded for being the bossy one. I honestly don't remember any incidents of my being bossy towards my siblings growing up, but I can site many in a week's time as an adult. I was a rule follower—obedient to a fault and rarely ever getting in trouble. My siblings saw me as a goody-two-shoes, but I was just too afraid of ever getting caught. Outside of my mouth getting washed out with soap once for accidentally biting my sister, I don't think I was ever grounded or reprimanded for much more than being "bossy". All it took was "the look" from Mom or Dad, and I never wanted to do anything bad ever again!

We all went to Mass every Sunday at the same church my mom grew up in, St. Anne's. Mom was Catholic, Dad was not. I think he went just to help her keep the four kids in line for an hour while she could practice being a good Catholic. Rarely a week passed when I didn't ask when we got in the car after Mass, "Mommy, Daddy, was I good today?" Most of the time they couldn't pin-point who was being fidgeting or chatty or otherwise misbehaved, so we all usually got the look. I would accept that during Mass, but I couldn't wait to verify my good standing once we were permitted to be ourselves again back in the car. If I didn't get the answer I wanted, I had to live with it, because anything else would be considered talking-back and I'd get much more than a disapproving look.

Mom was raised in Catholic schools and resented so much her being forced to conform to the strict rules and obedience of the Church that she resolved never to subject her own kids to such orthodoxy. We all went to public school, and therefore had to endure about ninety minutes of CCD every Sunday after Mass in order to receive our First Holy Communion and Confirmation. We were supposedly learning all the important truths, dogmas and practices of the Church, but all I got out of eight years of post-Vatican II CCD was "Jesus loves me". Not a bad lesson to learn, certainly, but a far cry from the foundation of faith I would need later in life to sort through inevitable trials with any sense of God's purpose or plan in them.

I'd say our childhood experience of the Faith was pretty much summed up in our prayer before dinner, our prayers of blessing for each family member (and pet) by name before bed, and our watching the annual three-night mini-series, *Jesus of Nazareth*, that aired on one of the three available TV channels on primetime television near Easter.

My high school years were filled with being a bubbly teenaged blonde rifle twirler in the marching band, trying to make sense of what it meant to "go with" boyfriends (that seemed to change each year with the passing of another grade), and adamantly disapproving of anyone who thought they were cool for drinking. I had a set of ideals already formulated in my mind—those being primarily whatever Mom and Dad said to do or not to do (to avoid any possibility of their disapproval), and anyone who fell short of those ideals was not worthy of calling themselves a friend of mine. Surprisingly, I did still have a set of very close co-ed friends all through high school, but they somehow managed to keep their differing ideals undetectable by me, and our friendships thrived just fine in my ignorance. Though my sister to this day remains in touch with many of her friends from high school, I was eager to move on to college, and never had much interest in looking back (aside from an occasional class reunion I attended out of sheer curiosity).

Never having any interest in a job or career outside the home, my only motivation for attending West Chester University was: 1) Mom and Dad were paying for it, 2) I would have, for the first time ever, "control" of my own life, and 3) where else would I find a husband? I am not joking when I tell you, when the guidance counselor presented me with a list of schools to consider for my higher education, the most influential school statistic was the ratio of boys to girls. Well, that, and West Chester had a marching band with a pretty impressive rifle squad; and it was only an hour away from Mom and Dad (just in case my new-found freedom became a little too much for me to handle or I had another trip to the emergency room—which I did—several times).

College proved to be not all that different for me than childhood or high school. I was still quite content to entertain myself and uphold my scrupulous ideals. Many nights throughout my freshman year ended with an hour or two of cross-stitching alone in my dorm room, watching Columbo or Star Trek (don't ask—I have no idea!) on my tiny portable TV while my roommate and co-ed dorm neighbors went to some wild off-campus party.

I met my all-time very best friend on my very first day of college. After Mom and Dad finished lugging all my new dorm room paraphernalia up to the sixth floor of Sanderson Hall, my complete-stranger roommate invited me to go to dinner with her and her high school friend who had a room just a few floors down. I accepted. In meeting her friend, I met Carolyn, the friend's new roommate.

Carolyn and I very quickly became the best of friends, and though I remained the perfectly contented hermit in my room alone at night, I never minded her loud, drunken intrusion on her way back into the dorm from a party, or holding her hair back while she threw up as she regaled me of all the fun I had missed. She accepted me for who I was, and I accepted her for who she wasn't. It was all a friendship was supposed to be, in my estimation.

By my second year I grew tired of "missing out" and I caved to the almighty drinking class. I spent the rest of my college career making up for lost time and enjoying losing my inhabitations that most people my age had been enjoying since freshman year of high school. I got tired of always being the good girl, and I was enjoying being somebody different. I was blissfully unaware of my faults and sins and content to be unaccountable for my ignorance and offenses.

Our friendship grew closer with each passing semester, and by our junior year, Carolyn and I rented an off-campus apartment together as roommates. It was also at that time I grew tired of studying during the day and drinking at night with nowhere I had to be in between, so I decided to pledge a sorority and add new people, places and things to my social calendar (always behind the status quo in when to start things). Carolyn was already a sister of a sorority for two years, and I really didn't want to be her shadow, so I pledged a different sorority, with her full encouragement and support. We enjoyed comparing our separate sisterhoods and though it required more time for us to be apart, it drew us even closer together.

She was the one who could laugh at me when I was angry or being unreasonable, and she was the one who could make me laugh any time I was overwhelmed with insurmountable woes. After long school breaks, we couldn't wait to reunite and fight each other for babble time about all that happened since the last time we were together. As soon as one would take a breath, the other would carry on where she had left off the last time she had taken a breath, and the conversation would continue for hours without missing a single detail from either account.

Our favorite times were getting ready to go to Pulsations, the local dance club for all who loved loud technotronic 90's music with an occasional 80's slow song with a potential suitor (dare I say future husband??). We had hundreds of inside jokes, and we laughed at them all the time—even to the point of being asked to leave class once. We could finish each other's sentences. We were kindred spirits. Sisters by choice. I trusted her and depended on her for every emotional high and low for four full years.

Sadly, college for us did not end in four years. We both had to go an extra semester to graduate. I, because I had changed majors in my second year; she for reasons I don't remember. I had started my freshman year in a field of study called "Communication Disorders", because I always had an interest in learning Sign Language and that seemed to be a logical name for a major that would cover such thing. I never actually asked anyone what kind of job I would have with a bachelor's degree in "Communication Disorders" because I never had an interest in getting a job after college. I just knew I had to choose something as a major so I could get through school and get on with my real life of marriage and motherhood.

I learned quite early on that "Communication Disorders" was code for "Speech Therapist" and it required way more commitment than I had any interest in giving; so I followed Carolyn's lead into "Elementary Education" instead. At least I saw some value in learning about childhood development and education since I was going to have kids of my own one day.

Our final semester was consumed with student teaching, and for Carolyn, a new fiancé. Her future life partner didn't exactly appreciate my need for her attention all the time, and she ultimately, in not so many words, had to make a choice. I lost. And one day midway through our final semester with grueling student teaching by day and waiting tables by night, she packed up my things while I was out and left a note asking me to leave. I called Mom—the one who was always there to solve every problem, and in less than an hour, Dad was there to rescue me. (I don't remember why Mom wasn't with him.) We packed up the car and went home to Lancaster. And Carolyn and I spoke maybe twice ever since. She sat two rows ahead of me at graduation and when the row between us was on the way up to the stage to be acknowledge, we caught each other's eye and said "I love you" and "I love you too", and that was the end of our friendship.

Four years of inside jokes and total dependency on each other, and in what seemed like an instant, it was all gone, just like that. It gutted me. And sometimes it still does. No one has ever filled the void she left in my life, and I'm pretty sure I protect it to ensure nobody ever will. Though we very likely have nothing in common anymore, and though no one could ever hurt me as much as she did that final semester of college, I still love her as "my very best friend", and sometimes I still miss her very much.

CHAPTER TWO

Fairy Tales And One Shining Knight

I think I was thirteen before my Dad could financially justify taking the six of us on annual summer vacations, and even camping in a pop-up camper a few miles inland from Rehoboth Beach, Delaware was a stretch. But we all thought we had died and gone to heaven "roughing it" at Four Seasons Campground in that damp, cramped home-away-from-home, with a kitchen table that converted into a bed, and a communal bathroom and shower house just a few steps away. That year was the first I had ever even seen the ocean, and every year I just couldn't wait to go back.

Rehoboth became our traditional family vacation spot, and for the four of us kids, it proved to hold some of our fondest memories. It was there that we "came of age" with our first taste of freedom—being allowed to take the four-mile trolley ride from the campground to the boardwalk and walk around town without Mom and Dad's constant supervision.

For my older brother, Brian, two weeks of family bonding in the great outdoors and only two weeks at the beach became too much for him to bear. After a couple years he managed to convince my parents to allow him to live there alone for the whole summer (which he did each year thereafter until he graduated college). By the time we'd get there the last week of July, he'd seem to have a kinship with everyone he worked with in FunLand, and he seemed to own the whole mile-long boardwalk that he'd proudly pound from one end to the next in his bare, black, calloused feet, as if only the "locals" could be so cool to do such a thing.

I was always a bit jealous, for I so loved the salty air and freedom of the beach, too! But it was a lot harder for Mom and Dad to trust their sheltered, fearless, naïve little girl to a town of strangers, over three hours away from home, than it was to trust their older, more worldly and mature son.

It was the summer just before my twenty-first birthday, after three years of proving to my parents I could survive collegiate life on my own, when Brian convinced them he would look after me and keep me safe for my last-chance summer with him at the beach. I couldn't wait to finish finals, pack my little silver Subaru with my full '80's-sized stereo system, all ten of my CD's and every piece of summer clothing that I owned. It was May 18th when I found my own way to my brother's large, empty, unfurnished, nearly-condemnable-condition rental house, just two doors off Rehoboth's boardwalk. Brian met me there and greeted me with the news that the house wasn't ready for residents—and wouldn't be for about five weeks. I didn't care. I was at the BEACH! I would've been content to sleep in my car and bathe in the murky salt water of the Atlantic Ocean all summer for all I cared!

Being the responsible big brother that he was, Brian used his can't say-no-to-him-charm to find a brand new condo where the owner would allow us to stay while we waited to get into the old mansion; but the condo, too, would be unavailable for another week or two. On to Plan C. There was a girl, Linda that Brian dated on-and-off over the summers in Rehoboth. She, her mom and her little sister lived there and worked at an ice cream shop they rented on the boardwalk every summer. Brian brought Linda home once during an off-season, so I had remembered who she was. Linda's mom loved Brian (as everybody did) so she made room for me in their rental beach home until the condo was ready. (To this day, I don't know where my brother or our rental-mates slept during that time, but all I needed to know then was that I was safe, my brother was nearby, and I was at the BEACH!)

I remember it as if it was yesterday. Brian walked me down the boardwalk to the ice cream shop to introduce me to Linda's mom. It was the middle of May, it was freezing, and there didn't seem to be a soul in town or on the boardwalk—but there was the ice cream shop, open and ready for business. Linda's family was Greek. They worked hard and were eager to serve anyone in need…even if their need was a soft-serve ice cream cone at ten o'clock in the morning on a cold, windy day at the beach.

And there he was—my future fairy-tale-dream-come-true—Linda's older brother, George, cleaning and assembling the cotton candy machine, wearing an old, worn-thin grey t-shirt that looked like he'd owned since the eighth grade. I thought he was just the hired help. I didn't know he was family, or that he would be sleeping under the same roof I would be that night.

A few weeks later, I was working alone in a tiny beach shop at the north end of the boardwalk (for someone else doing my brother a favor) when a strange man came into the store and started making passes at me and making verbal threats to lay me down on the beach and not let me up. I had never been in a situation like that before and I didn't know what to do. The cash register counter blocked my path to the door and I felt trapped. When he went into the changing room to put on a bathing suit three sizes too small to all but flash me when he came out, I called Brian, who came running down the boardwalk to make his presence known until the guy finally left.

As soon as he did, and Brian ran back to where he was working at the time, I locked the door to the beach shop and ran to the ice cream shop to ask where George was. He was back at the house, so I ran there next. I knew right then that George made me feel safe and protected—even more than my own big brother, who disappointingly never beat the guy up or threaten to kill him if he'd ever lay eyes on his little sister again!

The next morning, without my asking, as soon as I opened the beach shop door for business, there was George. He walked in, picked up a beach chair that still had a price tag on it to be sold, perched it right next to me at the cash register, and stayed with me the whole day to ward off anybody with any inkling of threatening me or making me feel uncomfortable again. My Knight in Shining Armor.

And so it began. We spent that summer of 1991 falling in love. It was the kind of summer romance you only ever see in movies or hear about in songs. I was the palest girl living at the beach. I worked all day every day in the beach shop, and all evening in Linda and George's family's ice cream shop. On the rare day or two I'd have off, I surprisingly left the beach and drove three hours to Baltimore to see George, where he and his dad kept their real home and family dog, Duke, while the girls lived at the beach all summer.

Unlike most of the movies and songs you hear of summer romances, ours survived the coming of Fall and another year and a half of college—an hour and a half apart from each other. It was just before the technology of email and cell phones became the normal mode of communication, so we spent hours talking on the phone and writing letters and making each other personal cassette tapes of the songs that made us think of each other. Sometimes I wonder how people fall in love any other way. "Absence makes the heart grow fonder" was a saying my mother used often. I hated it then, but really believe and value it now.

After college graduation, I moved to an apartment complex in Baltimore, just a few miles from George's family. It was the first time I ever lived completely alone. Still no interest in a "real career", I got a job as a teller in a bank, just buying time until George would ask me to marry him. One day while we were walking around White Marsh Mall, George spotted an eight-week old husky puppy in the pet store window. The puppy was pure white from head to toe, except for his pink nose and yellow Gatorade stain on his forehead. (They said it was normal for puppies to get a "cold", and the Gatorade was just helping him over it. Note to self: never believe anything anyone in a pet store in the mall tells you about puppies they're eagerly trying to sell to you.)

George fell instantly in love with that fuzzy ball of white fluff; and I, also easily taken by the cutest puppy ever, and eager to make George happy (and solidify our relationship), encouraged him to buy it and keep it at my apartment. By that time, I had moved from the apartment complex to a rented house with a yard while George continued to live in his family's home a few blocks away.

Living alone was still a novelty to me, and I was still reveling in my new-found freedom and control over my very own living space. Though I had no deep dark secrets or any reason to be so territorial, privacy and control were extremely important to me—so much so that I hadn't even given George a spare key to my apartment. I trusted him implicitly, but until we were married and sharing a home, I felt I had every right to control who and when people could enter my personal space.

George and I each had family dogs growing up, but apparently different models of how to potty-train them. George, being the perpetual defender of the weak, thought it best to protect the puppy with "a cold" from the cold harsh winter air outside and let him do his business on newspapers in "my" living room. And, instead of having to be on constant vigil or ever telling the pup "no", we should just rearrange "my" furniture to block him from places I didn't want him to go.

For the first time in my independent adult life, my "idealistic" temperament was being challenged. All I had ever known about raising puppies was what my parents had shown me when I was too young and disinterested to pay attention. And now, though having the long-longed-for freedom to make choices of my own, I had only my parents' ways, my parents' rules, and my parents' ideals to rely on in my thought process of discerning what was right and good for myself, "my" space, and "our" new puppy.

George won me over with his rationalization of how long a puppy can be expected to "hold it" during my long working hours, so I broke down and gave him a key to my apartment, "on certain conditions". Those conditions were explicitly drawn out to permit George, and only George, to come into my home without my being there, and to leave things as I had left them after he finished caring for "our puppy".

One day when I knew George was also working all day, I came home to fresh puppy cage with a not-so-fresh newspaper crumpled in my trash can. When I asked George who was in my home, he said his little sister. By all rational and compassionate thinking, I should have been grateful that Mellisa was willing and able to take such good care of my dirty and distressed little puppy while George and I were not able to, but I couldn't see it that way. All I could see was a relationship that tragically lost all trust, respect and communication, and though I had yet to be asked, I knew such a relationship could never lead to a happy marriage.

Three years into building a relationship with the man I knew after only weeks of knowing him would be my husband, came crashing down around me. I couldn't make him understand that it wasn't my desperate need for control that ruined us—it was his blatant disrespect of my personal boundaries. (Right, wrong or otherwise, they were mine, they were personal, and they were boundaries.) And I no longer trusted him to be my protector. In my mind, if he could disregard my boundaries in this matter, I wondered what other boundaries he would be capable of crossing in married life. I've always been black-or-white, all-or-nothing. If I conceded to his wishes over something that turned out to be so temporary and trivial in the long run, I just couldn't see how we would ever be able to build a marriage based on mutual love and respect.

There was no going back for me. He apologized many times in his "I'm not really wrong for doing what I did, but I really am sorry that you're bothered by it" way, but it wasn't enough to regain my trust. I sent him away (all the way to his parents' house a few blocks away), along with "our" puppy, the puppy cage and all the puppy toys. A few months later, when my lease expired, I returned, once again, to Lancaster—in an apartment still all my own, less than a mile from Mom and Dad. I was lost. For a year I fumbled around my life, wondering where to go and what to do next—devastated by the very real and obvious possibility that I may never be a wife and a mom, and even worse than that, the realization that George was no longer in my life.

Then one day I received a card in the mail. Written inside was this note: "Hi, Apollo told me that he missed his ma. So he wanted me to send you this card from him. He's getting bigger and stronger every day. Sometimes his leg bothers him, but he's alright. He also misses his big sister Skeeter [the cat George bought me when I first moved to Baltimore so I wouldn't be so lonely living all alone]. Tell her we both said hi, and give her a big hug from me too… Well, anyway we just thought we would write to say Hi. Hope everything is fine. Love, Apollo and George."

That, along with the lyrics to a song called "Desperado" by The Eagles, "You better let somebody love you before it's too late", made me realize that all loving, trusting, respectful marriages are worth fighting for. They're worth paradigm-shifting humility, compromise, and relinquished power and control to make them work. If we could find love and trust again even after a bitter and hurtful separation, then maybe all my dreams could still be possible…with the only man that ever had an active role in those dreams.

Our rekindled relationship was solidified with a three-day trip (for which I was "chosen" by mail to take) to Walt Disney World in Orlando with a one-night excursion cruise to the Bahamas. The cost was "discounted"—so long as we agreed to attend at least two painstaking presentations about the ever-so-convenient travel option known as "time-shares". George humored me, agreed to monopolize the "shared" driving time to and from Florida, and was thankfully unwavering in our not-so-mutual determination to leave Florida and the Bahamas time-share-less by the end of the trip. Through some honest heart-to-heart conversations on that trip, we came to an understanding that we really were meant to be together and we would have to learn new ways to communicate and protect our relationship as paradigms and ideals shifted on the road ahead.

But that didn't necessarily mean George was in any big hurry to get married. In his mind, marriage was for "old" mature people who were ready to have kids, and though he wasn't interested in being a perpetual bachelor or never being called "Dad", he just wasn't ready to take that next step on life's journey to "growing old together". He enjoyed being young and attached and without any real responsibility. Waiting for George to "be ready" was a true test of our resolve to work through disagreements together because, to me, every day that passed was another day I wasn't being a wife and a mom. I tried desperately to make him understand that we all live on borrowed time, and if I was going to die that next day, I wanted to die being his wife—not just his girlfriend; but that rationale didn't seem to motivate him in the least. He was just happy to have "his girl" back.

Finally, a year after our trip to Florida, in Rehoboth on an anniversary day-trip in May to where it all began, George got down on one knee and asked me to "be his girl forever" and put a ring on my finger. Though romantic in its own right, this, in George's mind, would simply buy him more time. In my mind, it was simply about time!

Two more excruciatingly long years I had to wait for my lifelong dream to come true. My wedding day just couldn't come fast enough, and I think I all but dragged my Dad down the aisle of St. Anne's as he seemed to begrudgingly take the smallest steps possible, supporting me with his military-style escort arm and holding my hand as if to hold onto his little girl as long as he possibly could. Though "church" to me was a place for not much more than socializing when I was growing up (right there in that very same church), and though I chose to do my socializing elsewhere when I was in college, in Baltimore, and in my independent adult life, I never considered getting married anywhere else. St. Anne's was home to me, and though the sanctuary lacked the mile-long aisle of the cathedral in The

Sound of Music that I imagined my Dad walking me down all my life, I always knew I'd be married there.

I remember beaming from ear to ear, and as I looked at the three-hundred-some adoring pairs of eyes sharing in my moment, I just couldn't wait to get close enough to see the look in my George's eyes. And finally, there he was. My knight. My fairy-tale-dream-come-true. In his eyes I could see he was a little overwhelmed with emotions of joy, pride, excitement and maybe just a little bit of fear. In that moment, there was no one else in the room. All I could see was our future in his eyes, and it was more than I ever dreamed it could possibly be.

The crowd reappeared in my consciousness as laughter broke when my stereotypically Greek soon-to-be mother-in-law approached the groom (with his bride finally at his side) to readjust the crooked collar on the back of his tux. It was just one of the moments that made our wedding day our own. Far different and better than being at the beach that fateful summer, nothing could ruin that day because…I was at the ALTAR!

The emotion of the day climaxed just before George and I exchanged vows. I mistakenly looked back at my Mom in a gesture of thanks for getting me to that point, then into the eyes of the man who loved me with an epic love, and if

I truly did not have one more day to live, I would have died happier than I ever dreamed I could be.

There was no stress in planning for that perfect day because as Mom said, "It's your wedding, but it's my party!" Mom handled everything. When it came to making decisions about flowers and invitations and cake decorations and centerpieces, she held up two choices and told me to pick one. As much as I had dreamt of that day, I had no interest in the details. I just wanted to marry that man and be his wife!

It really was a fun party, though, and we had a hard time discerning (according to the Emily Post book of etiquette Mom raised me on and referred to when setting the reception tables), when it would be an appropriate time to leave it. We had the bridal suite just upstairs from the reception hall reserved for the night, and we were anxious to begin our married life in it! It had been a long day, and I was so ready to be alone with my new husband. I didn't expect him to carry me over the threshold with my big bustled gown or anything, but I did expect the entrance to our married life to be a bit different than what awaited us behind that quintessential door.

Much to my dismay, the best man (George's cousin) was given access to the room before us, and he decorated it with what he and George found profoundly humorous. Instead of the rose petals any new bride would expect to see spewed about her sacred bridal space, there were dozens of condoms. A reminder that George was still, even on our wedding night, not ready to have kids. I was mortified. I always wanted and expected to get pregnant on my wedding night. What greater sign of our love for each other could there be than to conceive a child on the very day we consummated our marriage! Though I refused to let it darken the bright light of the day, I guess you could say the incident foreshadowed our less-than-romantic honeymoon.

That all-too-familiar less-than-apologetic attitude from my new husband lingered like the dark cloud that never seemed to leave the dreary skies of Martha's Vineyard that week. I had read (apparently not too closely) that you could go whale-watching on Martha's Vineyard (certain times of the year), and we thought that sounded like something newlyweds should do. We knew nothing about planning romantic trips, much less a honeymoon, and we (I) made every wrong choice. We ended up sleeping in a Bed-and-Breakfast that could very well have been used as the location for a New England horror film—complete with a freaky old guy squeaking up the deserted path on his old, creaky bicycle—and no TV, but a library filled with ghost stories of sailors past who still haunted the edifices of this fine honeymoon-nightmare-of-a-town, Martha's Vineyard. It was really that bad!

It was so bad that we left a day sooner than planned. We bought a house in York, PA a month before our wedding and we couldn't wait to move in and make it our home. We knew nothing about York. All we knew was it was between Lancaster and Baltimore, and we could feasibly get to both of our families on Christmas Day. I also knew I needed a town that would be just ours—a buffer from any unannounced visits, knowing full well that this home would be very different from the personal fortresses I had grown accustomed to, and I would need time and space to adjust.

Though both of us had jobs, we were not on any lifelong path to stay with them. I guess we figured everything would all work out, so we went for work wherever the wind blew us. I think between the two of us we had about six different jobs within our first two years of marriage. Actually, the week we returned from our honeymoon, that wind blew us to two different training programs, mine in Pittsburgh and George's in New Jersey. That, and not having a chain-link fence erected yet for Apollo to join us from my in-laws' house, made our new life together quite different than anything either of us had ever imagined.

CHAPTER THREE

All In

About two years after the less-than-ideal start to our marriage, George finally secured a decent-paying full-time job at a kitchen cabinet and furniture sales store just two blocks from our house (that he ended up keeping for thirteen years), and I was working a full-time job in the call center of the local cable company.

Apparently that perceived job and income security was what George was waiting for because when I asked if we should see a doctor about why we weren't getting pregnant, he didn't object. We weren't doing anything over those first two years of marriage to avoid pregnancy (aside from George's sheer will and hopeful thinking to keep it from happening yet), so with each month that passed it became harder and harder to justify God's reasons for having us wait.

Looking back, that was my "Eve in the Garden moment". Though everyone knows Satan as being the conductor of grand events of evil (like Auschwitz and 9/11) these events are not Satan's most prized accomplishments. His most powerful weapon is the *subtle* twist of God's truth in our everyday thoughts and decisions. Satan is the King of Lies, but even the most evil and diabolical lies are based on truth.

Satan—originally an angel of God named Lucifer, whose name meant "Bearer of Light"—turned away from God and became masterful at masking evil in things that *appear good*. I had to believe that I was a good person… I was kind to strangers, I helped people who needed help, I worked hard, I respected my elders, I honored my husband, I believed in God and I wanted to follow his commandment to be fruitful and multiply. And how could wanting babies in a loving, sacramental marriage be anything but good? I see now it wasn't in these thoughts alone that I erred. It was in trusting that my overall "goodness" and "good intentions" *justified* the path we were about to take—the path that proved to be against God's will.

Though discerning God's will was never high on my list of priorities, I still had an innate desire to please Him—or at least to never offend Him. But unfortunately, the will of God has always been just out of my reach. The Church attributes that to the Original Sin of Adam and Eve in the Garden of Eden. Just like Adam and Eve, though there were certain truths that I knew without doubt—like God's being a loving father, and Jesus' being His Son who loved me too—many "truths" as I understood them to be often seemed contrary to other "truths" as I understood them to be. To this day, I still often get confused in my thoughts and either run away from the conflicting subject all together, or I pick whichever truth is more comfortable for me to live with. And Satan wins, just like he did in the Garden of Eden.

Running away from my dream of being a mom was never an option, so I justifiably had to pick the latter option—choosing the truth that was more comfortable for me to live with. The only truth I knew was it was so *obvious* it was God's will for me to be a mom (since He's the one who put that desire in my heart since I was about two years old), so I concluded (with Satan's subtle trickery) that God must be asking me to trust him and seek the guidance of a fertility doctor. And there was the fallen Bearer of Light's twist. The truth Satan anchored his lie on was that God was asking me to trust Him. Satan's twist was to take matters into my own hands.

I had heard about a local infertility center in York with a doctor who was compassionate, knowledgeable and successful at treating couples who struggle with getting pregnant. George agreed to go with me to check it out. We both expected to be examined, but then ultimately be validated in our belief that nothing was really wrong with us, and that we would simply have to continue waiting for God's timing to be "right".

In our initial visit, they told us George would have the "easy" test. All he had to do was produce a semen specimen from which they could get a sperm count to determine how viable his reproductive system would be in the procreation process. And I think they even chuckled when they said, "And what man wouldn't be happy to do that?" Without going into graphic detail, they said I was permitted to help him by all means to reach this end. The process already felt vile and unnatural to me (especially in a business facility in a dark room that was apparently only ever used for this purpose), but I really believed God was asking me to trust Him, and that He would take care of everything if I could just do this.

That's how Satan is so masterful at twisting God's truth and love for us. God would never ask me to do something vile or unnatural—it's completely against the essence of His being which is love—but with my little-to- non-existent formation in God's truth, it was easy for Satan to trump God's will with my own agenda.

Testing on me, they warned, would be a little more complicated, and invasive. I was pricked many times for blood tests; but worst of all, I endured an inhumane procedure that they called a hysterosalpingogram. (They had to conceal the evilness of it in a long name that no one could remember, spell or pronounce!) It involved a camera being inserted between my legs, past the cervix, through the uterus and into each fallopian tube to determine if they were "open" to receive an egg during ovulation. All this while I laid—fully awake and unmedicated—on a cold, hard metal bench, tears streaming down my face, while George's hand turned blue from my grip. And worse than the unfathomable pain was the feeling of being utterly violated—physically, spiritually and emotionally. And still I convinced myself that this had to be God's will and that He had to be asking me to trust Him.

More repeatedly invasive tests followed for several months and again, moving slowly, gradually and subtly, Satan hooked us in his lies by increasing our hopes and expectations that certainly, after having made all this effort to trust the God who "helps those who help themselves" we would conceive a happy, healthy baby and it would all be worth it. Ultimately, they found no reason for concern in George's sperm count, and a low estrogen level was all they could find wrong with me. Actually, the way they put it was my estrogen level was "slightly lower than what they've found in women who have gotten pregnant." To me that meant I could still get pregnant; and that was all I needed to know.

With what I considered to be good news, we still decided to better our odds by my taking a drug designed to increase estrogen. This drug, however, was known to make vaginal fluid much thicker than normal and very difficult for sperm to penetrate; so, to get the best results, they recommended insemination. During this procedure, the doctor would inject my husband's sperm into me by way of a special syringe, bypassing the vaginal fluid all together.

This process, of course, had to begin in that vile, dark, unnatural room. Then it proceeded by removing all aspects of romance and intimacy (that God intended for the very purpose of procreating) by having a strange man inject a syringe into my vagina and uterus to manually eject my husband's sperm into me. Though I clung to the hope and expectation that this was God's plan and that this was going to work, I still left that office feeling numb, dirty, and violated. As I write and remember these feelings, I am amazed at how ignorant I could be to Satan's control over me through this time in my life! God is LOVE! Never could anything that made me feel numb, dirty and violated come from Him!

A few weeks later, I could hardly wait to go back to the fertility center for a blood test that would confirm my belief that this had to have worked—that I was pregnant and all my dreams were about to finally come true. It never really even crossed my mind that these efforts and emotional turmoil could result in anything else. I did everything I thought God was asking me to do. Surely He would reward me for my sacrifice, trust and faith in Him! But God cannot be manipulated—even by a loveable child with a big smile and hopeful heart that longs so deeply to love and to please Him. What follows is what I have since learned about God—all of which perhaps would have been lost on me if He hadn't allowed me to experience this test of his faithfulness through infertility.

"I AM". That is the name God gave himself. "I", meaning He is a being—one who can contemplate and understand the true meaning of identity; "AM" meaning all that exists. He is the one true God. He is the soul creator of all that exists—all of Heaven, all of Earth, and all that "is". He knows all, He is all-powerful, and He is everywhere. God created all things, rules all things, and can do *anything*. That means He not only created me, but He knew me—intimately—and He knew my deepest desire to have babies. It also means that He and only He—the one and only life-giving Creator of All could make us conceive—not the life-forcing hand of a fertility doctor.

I learned that God is eternal. There never was a time, nor will there ever be a time, when God doesn't exist. God is the creator of time itself; therefore He is not subject to it. He is transcendent. God simply is. He has no future or past, no beginning or end; and He does not change. So what was it to the Creator of Time to have us wait a few more months or years to have babies? *In God's time* all would be worked out just as it should be, governed by nothing but His love for me and His deepest desire for my true joy, happiness, and well-being.

I learned that God is almighty. His power is infinite and cannot be diminished or conquered. God is holy and good. He is not the source or cause of evil—evil abounds in the world because the world is fallen and broken. But believing in God's almighty power did not mean I would not suffer. Jesus tells us in John 16:33, "In the world you will have trouble, but take courage, I have conquered the world." "Trouble" meant big-time trouble, that swallowed me up and made me question if there even was a God, let alone a God who loved me. But He promised that if I would "take courage", He would conquer this trouble in my life. Suffering and evil exist in life because of the gift of free will that God gave us. He gave me free will because it is only with my free will that I can *love* him. And I can only love Him by trusting Him. He knew I would fall. He knew I would allow evil to control my thoughts and actions, but still, to Him my choosing to love Him instead was worth the risk of giving me that choice.

I learned that God always uses the worst things in our broken world for eternal good, and God paints on a canvas bigger than we can see or understand. Though my circumstances at the time made me question the power, the will and the love of God, I ultimately had to trust that He would use my suffering for my eternal good and for His own glory. Above all else, God is Love. In love, He sacrificed his own son to repair what I had broken—my trust in Him. Jesus proved through his Passion and crucifixion that if we trust the Father in all things, He will sanctify our suffering and use it for a greater good than we can even imagine.

Finally, I learned that God is merciful and loves me just the way I am—in all of my ignorance, brokenness, weakness and sin, He loves me. Just as any father loves his child—no matter how many poor decisions they make, no matter how disrespectful they are to him, no matter if they keep in touch—a father loves his children. I came to know God in these ways by considering the attributes of any good father. A good father is gentle, loving, protective, wise, supportive, encouraging, authoritative and trustworthy. A good father provides for his children, he listens, he gives good advice, commands respect, and inspires his children to be better. A good father has integrity, does what he says he will do, and he rewards his children for a job well done. Though I injured my relationship with God by choosing to accomplish my own agenda without any respect for His will, I knew my Father still loved me. If not, He could've destroyed me at any moment.

Still, I expected my reward. Certainly He had to have seen how much faith and trust I put in Him each trip I took to that fertility center, and certainly He would have to smile on me and say, "Daughter, well done!" So maybe He had his reasons for having us try insemination twice. Maybe some sort of chemical or hormonal change had to happen that just needed a little more time. That's what I believed when I continued to forge ahead with my own ambitions. Despite God's whisper in my soul that everything about this was still so vile and far from His life-giving will, we tried insemination a second time the following month. And again my heart was shattered. My efforts to sacrifice and trust according to my own will and agenda produced no baby—no smile from God, no "Job well done". Just failure, emptiness, denial and rejection.

The failed second insemination was much more rejection than I could handle. I couldn't do it anymore. Apparently this was not exactly what God needed me to do to conceive a child—if it was, it would've happened by then. I was at a loss. And when I'm lost, I give up. My only option left was to leave our ability to bear children in God's hands (where I should have left it from the beginning). I figured if He wanted me to get pregnant, He certainly had the power to make it happen naturally so there was no sense in enduring any more vile procedures. So we moved on—hoping, trusting, and enjoying the "practice" of the sacred, loving, intimate embrace that, by God's design, was created for conceiving babies.

One final note I'm compelled to make about this trial in my life: I have since learned we cannot just excuse away every error we make to our unwitting bequest of a bad choice some mythological couple made in the beginning of time. Our redemption depends on the effort we make to choose *rightly*—that is to choose in ways that are compatible with the will of God—even when (*especially* when) those choices conflict with our own agenda. It absolutely requires God's grace; it absolutely requires our cooperation with that grace, and it absolutely takes love and trust in a Father who makes good of all things.

Chapter Four
Bring on the Rain

Through our life-building years together, George didn't know me as a church-going woman or an extremely faith-filled person, and we were both content with that. George and his family were Greek Orthodox, but they kept their faith where I kept mine—somewhere in the deep caverns of our hearts, to hold onto as some sort of "emergency kit" if ever we needed it. Our life was good—back on track from the ups and downs of infertility treatments, and just happy to be building a home and life together. There were no emergencies, no pressing need in our hearts to practice the quiet, unnourished deep-seeded faith we were raised on, or for God in our daily life.

We were in our third year of marriage, we were both thirty-one years old, and our hearts were open and ready and longing for whatever life had in store for us.

And then it happened! All my longing, all of my emptiness, all of the lack-of-purpose and meaning in my life was finally acknowledged, heard and answered! But not the way I expected it to be. The answer, instead, was that inevitable "emergency".

One evening in early November 2001, during an intimate moment of being one with each other, the simple enjoyment of being husband and wife with high hopes for conceiving a baby God's way suddenly turned into something much less romantic. George noticed a strange lump in my left breast that felt hard—like two knuckles poking out of my chest wall. Though it didn't occur to me right away to start panicking (it's always taken me a while to process things), as the night set in, it started to dawn on me that there was a very real possibility that I could have breast cancer.

All I knew about breast cancer was that it was curable, so I thought even if that's what the lump would turn out to be, it couldn't be that big of a deal. (Ignorance is bliss, as they say.) Even with that in mind, though, I couldn't help but think of the people I knew with other cancers, all of who had died. They all endured debilitating effects of chemotherapy that only left them pale, thin, weak, and eventually dead; so that was all I could think about that evening—death. Could I really be dying? I was only married three and a half years, I had no children, and I hadn't made my mark on the world yet. Surely, I couldn't die before I made my mark, could I?

The next day, I went to my HMO Primary Care Physician's office. This was not a doctor who knew me or my family or our medical history. I had seen him once previously for a stiff neck and once for a lump under my other arm that turned out to be a cyst. Though he was convinced what we were feeling was a common condition found in women my age that was typically benign and not at all harmful, he referred me for a mammogram to be certain. If the mammogram was to be inconclusive, they would do an ultrasound and I'd get the results right away. If there would still be doubt, they would do a surgical biopsy. The doctor really believed that was the most I would have to endure, and in the end I would be just fine.

By that evening, I was convinced he was right. I had the experience of a doctor to assure me I did not have cancer, so it seemed silly to worry about it any longer. I figured any tests or procedures I would have to go through to deal with the lump paled in comparison to a breast cancer diagnosis, so that night I rested peacefully.

The earliest we could schedule the mammogram and ultrasound was that Friday, late afternoon. With shades of doubt resurfacing in my mind, I left work at the cable company early the day before "to prepare myself" (and ended up not going back until six months later). My appointment Friday was for 3:45 at Apple Hill Medical Center. George came with me. I had never gotten a mammogram before. I thought women didn't have to do that until they were forty. I had just turned thirty-one in September. When I was called back to change into a gown and to take a seat in the inner waiting room, I saw another woman there. She was looking so nervous, like something was terribly wrong. I, on the other hand, was feeling very calm so I figured I must be fine—if I weren't, I would have been looking like she did. My attitude was that I was only there to appease the doctor and my mother—I wasn't there because I really believed anything was very wrong.

I was called into the room where the mammogram machine was (by a woman who was obviously anxious to get out of work for the weekend) and was asked a bunch of questions I couldn't answer, like, "How old was your grandmother when she died of breast cancer?" (I was a year old, but she was never one to tell her age), and, "How old were you when you got your first period?" I couldn't even tell her when my last period was, let alone my first. She continued by asking if I could be pregnant. I'm sure she wasn't prepared for my tragic little story about our infertility issues, but I had to be completely honest. Ultimately I answered, "Yes, I suppose it is *possible* I could be pregnant, but I don't see why this month would be any different than the last thirty." My longwinded answer left her questioning the risk of a mammogram (which is apparently harmful to babies), so she left me alone while she went to consult the doctor.

When she returned, she said the doctor wanted me to do the ultrasound first then from there decide if a mammogram would still be needed. The ultrasound technician first applied a warm gel to my breast then slid the camera around, pressing into my breast from all different angles as she pressed a button on the computer keyboard that snapped the pictures. The procedure took about 15 minutes, after which the doctor came in and asked me to look at the monitor screen as he explained what we saw. There was obviously something there. It was black in the center with what looked like gray cement around the edges. He said if it would have been pure black like the background, it would have been a cyst. This, though, was abnormal in shape and had gray in it, which told him there were solid characteristics to it.

Based on those results, he opted for the mammogram. The mammogram machine had two horizontal plates, which pressed together with my breast clamped between them. The technician had applied adhesive metal "markers" to each of my nipples which would indicate on the pictures the exact location of the lump in respect to my overall breast. After the technician took a couple pictures, she had me wait alone there for five to ten minutes while she processed the film for the doctor. There, alone, in a cold, dark, unfamiliar room, it had begun to occur to me there might actually be a problem. Maybe the HMO doctor was wrong. Maybe it was right for me to be scared.

The technician came back and directed me back to the changing room, then I was reacquainted with my husband. When we walked together into the conference room, all my x-ray and ultrasound pictures were hanging up on the wall. With an untrained eye, even I could recognize the lump; but what I did not recognize were the thousands of little white "shattered glass" fragments the doctor called calcifications, which were all through the lower half of my breast. It was the appearance of all those calcifications that concerned him most; and all in all, at the end of the conversation, he said he'd be very surprised if they would prove not to be cancer.

That was 5:00 PM Friday afternoon. There was no one available to turn to with questions or to tell us where to be or what to expect next. George and I were on our own for the weekend to consider the worst. All we were given was a name and phone number of a breast cancer surgeon to call first thing Monday morning for the earliest appointment available. Things were moving very fast. Just that morning I was feeling safe and assured that nothing bad was happening to me, and now later that same day I was feeling very unsafe, vulnerable and desperate. If things could change so rapidly in one day, I couldn't bear the thought of what changes a whole week could bring.

That weekend I considered the fact that it could be the last weekend I would ever have two breasts. I felt a very real possibility that before the end of the week my left breast could be removed. I felt I needed to spend that time appreciating my body as it was while it lasted, and grieving for what it could very well become. It was like being told someone very near to me was dying and I only had a few days to soak her up, love her, appreciate her and remember her for the way she was. I was afraid to think positively because if I did, I could potentially miss the only opportunity I might have to remember myself as I was.

It saddened me that weekend that I had nobody but family to turn to. I had no close girlfriends. Most of the time, I felt completely satisfied having my best friend in my husband, but there were other times I longed for the understanding and connection of other women. I missed Carolyn. How I wished to have her friendship back that weekend. I longed for her to cry with me and to make me laugh over something stupid, as she was always able to do. But it had been at least eight years since we had spoken and I didn't feel it would be fair of me to call her out of the blue with such devastating news. Then, just as I was thinking of her, one of our old favorite songs from our college days came on the radio. I thought it was a sign for me to call her, so I did. She answered the phone. I don't even think I said hi. I said, "It's Binky. I think I have breast cancer."

Though I had no right or reason to, I expected her to react the way she would have back in college, when she knew me and knew exactly what I needed. This, however, was a lifetime later, and things had changed. She was pleasant, thankfully, but she was not the girl I once knew. She replied with stories of women she worked with that had breast cancer and survived, and continued with an affirmation that science and technology had come a long way, and that doctors could do amazing things. Then the conversation became extremely uncomfortable, so I ended it quickly. (I had left her with my phone number, but I never heard from her again.) The rest of the weekend, I was more upset over that phone call than I was over the thought of breast cancer.

My parents came over later that afternoon. I held out about five minutes before looking in my Dad's eyes. He had spent most of my childhood working, but since I had moved away to college, I had learned he was a very sensitive and sentimental man. It broke my heart to see him cry for me and the circumstances I was facing. My mother, on the other hand, was always very determined to hide her emotions and very rarely did she ever let me see when she was hurting.

That day was no different. When she came in, she gave me a big hug and very matter-of-factly stated that no matter what would happen, we were all going to get through it together. According to her, even my younger brother, Kevin, who none of us had heard from in two years, was included, whether he liked it or not. She was not about to let cancer (or anything else for that matter) bring our family down.

Brian called that evening from Colorado. Through his tears, he told me he was not going to believe the worst until he heard the facts, and he wanted me to do the same. He and Kevin were more than brothers—they were the very best of friends, but even Brian hadn't heard from Kevin in two years. Still, Brian said he left Kevin a message about the family crisis (my pending cancer diagnosis), and it comforted me to know my whole family was pulling together to support me.

That evening, after all the doctors' appointments were over, my parents were gone, and the phone stopped ringing, I was alone with my George. I sat on his lap while he considered for a moment the idea of not having me around. As tears came to his eyes, he told me if anything happened to me, he would take good care of our pets and never move away from our home. Moments later he dried his tears, apologized for crying, and promised he would be strong for me. Little did he know, his tears gave me more strength than his promises did.

Monday afternoon (seven days after first feeling the lump) I was at the breast surgeon's office for a consultation and more tests. Our first encounter there was with an unsympathetic nurse who responded abruptly to my pessimistic questions with, "You won't lose your breast. Very few women need mastectomies anymore. If it's cancer, we'll do a lumpectomy and radiation and you'll keep your breast."

We waited for over an hour for the doctor and it was again very late in the afternoon when I endured my third test, a core needle biopsy. Without any sedatives to relax me, the surgeon shot my breast with a Novocain needle which was supposed to numb me for what came next. Using the ultrasound machine to locate the lump, the doctor proceeded to stick me four more times with a blunt needle that had a tiny scoop on the end which was used to extract tissue samples from the core of the lump. The Novocain was not helpful. He could not believe I was in enough pain to cause the tears streaming down my face until he realized afterward that he must have been hitting a muscle. At 6:00 PM the nurse bandaged me up and sent us on our way to wait another long three days for the results.

Over those three days, I received many phone calls offering me more support, including one from my long-lost little brother, Kevin. Brian also called again and told me he, his wife and three young sons would hop on a plane the moment I felt I needed them. I also I heard from old friends, and friends of friends I did not know but who had survived breast cancer and wanted to shed some light on the situation.

Hearing the phone ring gave me much needed strength during the day, but as I would lay down in the darkness and quiet of the night, my fears consumed me. Not only was the thought of death constantly lingering around, but I also wrestled with the fears I had of smaller things like having to get an IV in the back of my hand for surgery (something about that always bothered me), being wheeled away from my husband as I entered the operating room, and losing my hair. Waiting became most detrimental to my spirits—it only gave me time to consider the worst.

Day Ten, Thursday, November 15th, George and I were back at the breast surgeon's office to hear the results of the biopsy. The lump was over 80% cancerous. Though more tests were to be done to confirm the calcifications were also cancerous, I definitely had cancer; I most likely needed a full mastectomy of my left breast and six months of chemotherapy. I would lose my hair and we wouldn't be able to try for a baby again for at least two years. If I happened to be pregnant at that moment, the doctor said I would have to make a difficult decision and consider the life of the mother over the life of the baby. That was the most devastating news of all! I would *never* choose my life over my baby's!

There were three other people in the room discussing what tests to schedule, who would be my plastic surgeon and when I would have surgery. It hardly seemed they knew I was even in the room or that I was trying desperately to comprehend what I had just heard. All I remember saying was I wanted the surgery as soon as possible. I knew that if I had something to do, I just wanted to do it and get it over with so that I could move on. I had already learned that waiting was much too difficult for me and just putting it off wasn't going to make it go away.

From the breast surgeon's office, we were guided to a different suite of the complex for an x-ray of my lungs. I was still in a daze, but I think they said my lungs looked healthy enough to withstand surgery and chemotherapy. Before I was finally sent on my way, I still had to stop at another suite for a blood test. The last thing I wanted at that moment was another needle, but by that time, I no longer had any control over what happened to me. I felt like I was some sort of lab rat, drugged, dragged, poked and prodded with no power to stop any of it.

On the way home, I made George stop at St. Joseph Catholic Church (where I had been to Mass maybe once or twice for Christmas or Easter since we moved to York). I wept at the foot of the crucifix hanging on the wall and prayed for strength and grace to get me through the uncertain days and months ahead. It had been a long time since I had been to church, but I somehow felt safe there.

When I got home, I called Mom. She didn't react the way I thought she would when I told her I had breast cancer; in fact, she didn't seem to react at all. All she said was, "We've got NUNS!" A friend of hers had my name put on the prayer list at a convent somewhere and somehow that made my mom feel safe. Unfortunately, it did not have the same affect on me. I was still scared.

Day Eleven, I was in another foreign place getting an MRI. Though the use of MRI's was new to the field of diagnosing breast cancer, they were hoping to determine the malignancy of the calcifications without having to do another biopsy. The breast surgeon, the day before, promised me it would not be painful, but he apparently had conveniently forgotten about the needles the inexperienced technician had to use to insert a catheter into my arm into which they injected contrast dye for the test.

When the catheter was finally in place, I was taken to the MRI machine. I had never seen or experienced one of those before either. I was quite claustrophobic, yet nobody bothered to ask me if I was, and nobody bothered to inform me I could have taken sedatives and/or used the "open" MRI to ease my anxiety. I was enclosed in a full-length tube, on my stomach, face down in a pillow, with only about three inches of clearance to lift my head, for thirty minutes. The only thought that ran through my head the entire time was, *"He lied to me!"* Ultimately, the pain, anxiety and expense of the MRI proved to be inconclusive and I needed the second biopsy anyway. The breast surgeon had warned me of the different emotional stages I would go through, and he wanted to get me to the angry stage as quickly as possible. He succeeded.

My sister, Kim called later that evening. She refused to believe I had a potentially fatal disease. She was angry with me for not being positive. Kim had always been very determined to make good out of anything that was bad and had always been a great inspiration to me, but at that point, her optimism only made me feel hurt, angry, misunderstood and somehow wrong for feeling sorry for myself.

That weekend, I received many more phone calls. George had to work and I was home alone. The sound of the phone ringing became a great comfort to me. The one phone call that did me the most good was from George's cousin—the best man at our wedding. (I had forgiven him for the bridal suite incident by then.) He and I had been partners in several family dart-throwing competitions in the past and he called to conspire with me ways to use my upcoming surgery as a hustling tool. He had a way of making me laugh. He did not take pity on me or treat me with "kid gloves", but he acknowledged what was happening and let me know he cared.

That Sunday, George and I went to his parents' house in Baltimore for dinner. When we got there, my father-in-law was the only one home. We exchanged a kiss on the cheek as usual. No hug, no look, no acknowledgement at all of what was happening to me. A few minutes later, my mother-in-law came in with groceries. She stayed preoccupied with putting her purchases away and eventually asked if I was okay, expecting a "yes" for an answer. I didn't have the heart to tell her otherwise. Throughout dinner, conversation carried on as usual about work, the dogs and sports. I felt like I was invisible or in the twilight zone. Was I the only one who realized that I had breast cancer and was about to go through the trial of my life? I felt so rejected and unimportant. Finally somebody asked when I had my next doctor appointment; but then conversation reverted back to the same unimportant chit-chat.

After dinner, the rest of my husband's family stopped in after having been at a football game. Mellisa never entered the room where I was sitting. Linda and her husband made their rounds with kisses and proceeded to the dining room for dinner. I wanted to scream just to get somebody's attention! All of my in-laws had always been very loving and very caring towards me, so their actions (or lack thereof) surprised me and broke my heart. It wasn't that I wanted the whole evening to revolve around my circumstances—all I wanted were hugs or touches or looks that *acknowledged* something terrible was happening to me and that they were behind me. I realized later that breast cancer was not only scary to me, but everyone who loved me. They were afraid if they mentioned it at all, it would only upset me, and seeing me cry would be too much for them to bear.

About a week after my initial diagnosis, I met the plastic surgeon. He reviewed my options for breast reconstruction. The first decision I had to make was whether or not I even wanted reconstruction, then if I did, I had to decide between immediate reconstruction done at the same time as the mastectomy, or waiting until some later time for another surgery to reconstruct a new breast. The third decision I had to make was if I chose reconstruction, which of the following would I use to build the new breast: an implant, muscle tissue from my back or muscle tissue from my abdomen. I had five days to decide, as my surgery was already scheduled for November 27th—hardly enough time to research, ask questions or make a difficult decision that would affect the rest of my life.

Directly from the plastic surgeon's office, I went to Apple Hill for the second biopsy (called a stereo tactic core needle biopsy), which would definitively determine the malignancy of the calcifications, as well as the necessity to follow through with the mastectomy. This procedure seemed quite complicated. I had to lie on my stomach on an elevated metal table with my breast hanging down through a hole. Under the table was a mammography machine, which clamped my breast in place. This time I had taken Tylenol PM® to take the edge off and the breast surgeon gave me four times the Novocain as the last time, so I really didn't feel much pain. This needle had more of a tube than a scoop on the end, with a knife that sliced through the tissue and secured the tissue while it was being removed. He took twelve samples, eleven of which were full of calcifications. That evening, when the Novocain wore off, I was very sore. My instructions were to tuck a small ice pack in my bra and leave it on all night as I slept—as if my comfort had not been sacrificed enough already.

I spent the next five days celebrating Thanksgiving, recuperating from the biopsy and trying to prepare for what lied ahead. Thanksgiving was very emotional for me. I had watched the Macy's Thanksgiving Day Parade every year of my life and George begrudgingly adapted to the tradition when we got married. As we watched it that Thanksgiving morning, I broke down in tears several times wondering if that would be the last time. Thanksgiving dinner was back at my in-laws. This time it was much different. My father-in-law even said a very special and endearing blessing, which was completely out of his character, asking God to guide the hands of my surgeons and to keep me safe. It brought tears to my eyes (and his). Aunts, uncles and cousins came, all shedding tears and sharing hugs. All the attention consumed me and made me feel like I could endure anything. I had love, so I knew I would be okay, no matter what happened.

To finish out the weekend and to continue with every never-more-important holiday tradition, Kim picked me up bright and early for Black Friday shopping. I was still very sore from the last biopsy and I tired quickly, but it was well worth it to feel somewhat normal and to spend quality time with my sister.

CHAPTER FIVE

A Kiss on the Hand

The day before my surgery was scheduled, I went to the breast surgeon's office to find out, with no uncertainty, that the calcifications were indeed cancerous and there was no backing out. From there I went into work to tie up loose ends. Luckily, I was eligible for short-term disability, which would pay me 75% of my base wages for up to six months. I submitted that paperwork, referred my pending work to my supervisor and said my goodbyes.

When I got home, I did the laundry, washed the dishes, dusted, vacuumed, cleaned the bathroom and went to the grocery store to fill the refrigerator. I was expecting guests to come stay with our new puppy, Jedi (Apollo and Skeeter had since passed) and offer my husband moral support, so I had to make my house look perfect. I also called my parents and in-laws with directions to the hospital, and asked each to call certain people in particular with any news of my progress. I packed for a possible five day stay at the hospital. I did not allow myself to consider what was going to happen to me the next day. In fact, I brainwashed myself into believing it was the night before my wedding—I was anxious, people called me to tell me good luck, they loved me and they'd see me tomorrow, and I did not sleep well. It worked. I didn't cry once.

The next morning (Day 22, five days after Thanksgiving) I was expected at the hospital at 5:45 AM. The breast cancer surgeon came in at 7:00. He had explained to me in his office previously that during the mastectomy he would remove several lymph nodes from under my arm (what they called sentinel node mapping) to determine if the cancer had spread beyond my breast. He would remove four lymph nodes to start then send them to the lab where it would be determined if they contained any signs of cancer. He would then complete the mastectomy and get word from the lab if he should remove any more nodes (called an axillary dissection). If cancer would not be detected in any of the first four nodes, it would give us some certainty that the cancer had not spread or metastasized anywhere else in my body. The prognosis would get worse if the number of cancerous nodes increased. To aid in this process, the breast surgeon had to inject a blue dye directly into my breast an hour before the surgery was to begin, this time with no Novocain. He used four different needles, which were of course very painful, and the dye left my breast burning. I could not wait to be put to sleep!

As I was waiting to go to the operating room, George, my parents, my sister and a friend of the family stayed with me. I was determined to just go through the motions and stay unemotional because I knew if I started crying, I would not be able to stop. I was getting angry because my "moral support" did not have the same determination I did. Around 9:15 I was wheeled down the hallway with George holding my hand and my entourage following (and crying) behind me. When we got to a set of double doors, they were asked to stay behind. Thankfully I had already been somewhat sedated, and the nurse continued to ask me questions, so George's kiss goodbye on the hand was not as traumatic as I had imagined.

The operating room was extremely cold. I was introduced to the surgical team, most of who were already donned in their surgical caps and masks. I remember one of them was wearing an American flag bandana in honor of those lost on 9/11 in the World Trade Center (just a couple months before). It gave me peace and reassurance knowing I was in the hands of someone who truly had a heart and compassion for others. I was asleep just moments later.

The entire surgery was about five hours long. I had opted for immediate reconstruction with the muscle from my back (called the latissimus dorsi). I was not comfortable with the idea of an implant for several reasons. I had heard a lot of horror stories about implants; and if I chose to get one, it could create an infection, or my body could reject it, and it would have to be removed. Even if all went well, breast implants required two separate surgeries. The first would involve inserting a devise that would work like a balloon. For weeks following the initial surgery, I would have to make trips to the plastic surgeon's office to pump it up until it reached the size of my other breast. At that point, the second surgery would involve removing that balloon-like device and inserting the actual implant. My other reconstruction option was to use the muscle and fat from my abdomen (referred to by my plastic surgeon as being similar to a "tummy tuck"); but this method was not recommended if I ever wanted to conceive and carry a baby for nine months.

With only five days to make my decision, I felt certain I would feel like a freak if I woke up from surgery with only one breast; so by process of elimination, I chose the latissimus dorsi flap from my back. It was my own bodily tissue which would cause no risk of rejection and the only downfall would be a scar below my left shoulder blade. I could live with that. I may have made different decisions if I had more time to research my options, but under the circumstances, I felt I did the right thing.

I remember waking up in the recovery room absolutely freezing! I had four warmed blankets on me and I still could not stop shivering. It felt more like violent convulsions than shivering to me, and I was afraid I would reopen my incisions or somehow ruin what the surgeons had just accomplished.

The next thing I remembered I was in a private room with George sitting by my side, holding my hand once again. There were what felt like blood pressure cuffs on each of my legs, being automatically pumped by some machine, and I had a button in my hand to press when I felt I needed more morphine. There were three drainage tubes hanging from my left side, collecting excess fluid that my body could not process. I was surrounded by close friends and others were consistently coming in and out of the room, offering me and George unsolicited, yet much appreciated, support. All in all, my spirits were pretty high. I focused on getting well rather than considering what I had lost.

Later that evening, the breast surgeon stopped in with the results from the sentinal node mapping and axillary dissection. One of the first four lymph nodes he removed during surgery was found to have cancer and as an added precaution, he removed thirteen more, all of which were found to be cancer-free. Out of four breast cancer stages,

Stage IV being the worst, mine was classified as Stage II. I stayed in the hospital three days. George stayed with me every night, and my mom took his place each day so he could go home to rest and visit the puppy. Throughout the day, my mom kept track in my cancer case of every visitor, card and gift I received so that I could thank each person properly when I was feeling better. I was so grateful she took the initiative to do that for me.

By day three in the hospital, I was feeling good about being there. I loved the attention. I loved having my husband by my side holding my hand. I loved hearing my mom's stories of who said what about me and who was praying for me. I loved being able to control the bed to make it comfortable each time I had to move. I loved having the bathroom two steps away. And I loved having nurses consistently in and out of my room bringing me medicine, emptying my drainage tubes and asking if I was okay. I did not want to leave. I did not want to be responsible for taking care of myself and I did not want George or my family to attempt to do the things the nurses were trained to do.

The doctor said I would be able to stay one more day, but a couple hours later a different doctor came in to inform me my insurance company saw no purpose in my staying any longer. I began to panic. Just as I was beginning to feel safe, my world was once again being turned upside down. In the hospital I could focus on healing and soaking up all the attention. At home, I would consistently be reminded I could not do the things I was used to doing on my own, like the laundry, the cooking, the cleaning and playing with the puppy. I had always been very independent, especially when it came to taking care of my home and my family. I was not ready to be put in a position where I would have to ask for help. I became numb and George and my parents began buzzing around me, packing up my things and preparing me for the ride home. I was discharged and home on the couch within the hour.

In the days to follow, George took care of all the household chores, my mom came to dote on me when George had to go back to work, and a visiting nurse came once a day to empty my drainage tubes and clean and check my incisions for infection. Three days after being home, I had a follow-up appointment at the plastic surgeon's office. He removed one of the three drainage tubes and the staples he used in place of sutures around my breast and under my arm. The other two drainage tubes would have to stay in another three days. By then, the visiting nurse had stopped coming so I was responsible for emptying my own tubes and cleaning my own incisions. This was extremely difficult for me, especially since I did not have the strength or courage to even look at my mutilated body until weeks later. Thankfully, I had a husband, family and friends to help.

At my follow-up appointment with the breast surgeon, even though he told me my shoulder would be extremely stiff and painful from surgery, he yanked it up in the air to see how far it would go, leaving me fighting with every ounce of my being not to kick him and scream out in pain. (After the release of Mel Gibson's The Passion of the Christ, I have since related that jolt to the Roman soldier's yanking Jesus' arm over to reach the hole that was pre-marked for the spike that would hold him to the cross.) He also felt the need to drain the two remaining tubes hanging from my side and was not especially gentle with that process either. Emotions started kicking in and I could not take one more pain.

He finally eased off and showed me how to "walk the wall" with my fingers to rebuild the range of motion in my shoulder. He instructed me to stand with my face to the wall, raise my arm as high as I comfortably could, then take three more "steps" up the wall saying, "Damn you doctor!" (That part seemed to come easy to me!) I was to do ten "walks", four times a day until I could quickly raise my arm all the way with no pain or hesitation.

Emotionally, I had good days and bad days. For the most part, I thought I stayed pretty strong, but when I would start to cry for one little pain, tears flowed continuously for every "full-body-blow" pain and emotion I held in since the last time I had cried. George had a hard time understanding why I would get so emotional over one little thing, but what

I could not make him understand was every little thing built up to several big things. I was still having a hard time coming to grips with the fact that I had cancer—a disease that could ultimately kill me. Before surgery, I felt completely normal and healthy; I didn't *feel* sick. After surgery, I only felt mutilated. If only I had had time to come to terms with the ramifications of being diagnosed with cancer, I may have been able to accept what the surgeons did to me more easily.

One night in particular, I had reached my lowest low. It happened about a week and a half after being home from the hospital. I was still in pain from surgery and that night I had an intense pain in my legs (which was a normal occurrence throughout my lifetime when I was feeling tired or stressed) that became overwhelmingly unbearable. While panicking and starting to hyperventilate, I prayed to God he'd let me die that night in my sleep. I could not take any more. I told George what I had prayed for. He took it extremely personally that his love for me was not enough to make me want to stay alive. I tried to tell him I will always feel his love from heaven, and he mine, but it was not helping him feel any better. It was a terrible position to put him in, but at that moment, my anguish was just too much to bear. I took medication to calm me down. It kicked in about 10-15 minutes later and I finally fell asleep. When I woke up the next morning I no longer had the pain in my legs, and my emotional state was much better. That was the only time through my entire ordeal I ever wished to be dead.

Three weeks after my surgery, I made love to my George for the first time. I had been dreaming of him the whole night before, and when I woke up, all I could think about was being near him. No thoughts of surgery, pain or my mutilated body entered my mind…only the longing for a deep connection with the man I loved. It was beautiful and magical as it always had been, and it made me feel so loved and so close to him. But even though that morning did a world of good for me, it did not mean I was ready to get physical at any given moment. I still struggled immensely with my body image and sexuality for months to come and there were many times I pushed George away. Thankfully, he remained understanding, patient and willing to give in to me whenever I decided the moment was right again.

In the midst of my recovery was Christmas. In addition to needing rest, I also needed to make my treasured traditions of the holiday feel normal. Included in those traditions was attending a family Christmas breakfast sponsored by my Dad's Lions Club. I was on the verge of crying the whole time I was there. When different people came to see how I was doing, I didn't know if I should tell them the truth or if I should tell them everything was okay, just to spare their feelings. At one point during breakfast, I snapped at my Mom for continuing to talk about my situation. I so desperately needed to focus on something else that morning. I knew if the conversation continued to revolve around me, I would end up in tears. Funny how I my needs changed from that first dinner with my in-laws to now. That's the way it was with my emotions throughout the whole time I was being treated for cancer—one minute I was up, the next minute I was down, and in each minute I expected my family to grab onto that emotional rollercoaster ride and give me what I needed without any complaint or mistake.

Another Christmas tradition involved planning and hosting a family pre-Christmas ornament exchange party, which involved fully decorating my house, planning games, shopping for trinkets to use as prizes and fixing all the food. For that evening, I chose to stop taking pain medication and to have a couple of cocktails instead. I told each of my guests as they arrived that I was not sick that evening and we were not going to discuss it. Everyone had a good time, including me, and I was so proud of myself for pulling it off.

Christmas Eve, we went to my in-laws. There was news. Linda showed us a card she gave her parents earlier that evening, signed by "Baby". She was pregnant with the first grandchild of the family. She had gotten pregnant on her honeymoon three months earlier. No words can describe the flood of mixed emotions that hit me in that moment. That night when we got home, all I wrote in my journal was "She's having a baby…and I'm having chemo."

It seemed so unfair. George was the oldest of the family, and we had been married over three years more than Linda had. *We* were supposed to have the first grandchild. It was a very difficult position to be in, feeling (really) very happy for Linda and her new husband, and feeling so envious, jealous and betrayed all at the same time. Though it took a little while for me to see past myself and my own self-pity, that baby became the only thing I had to look forward to at the end of my journey through cancer. I could hardly wait to meet him and tell him he was a precious gift, given to me when I needed him most. He gave me hope, something to look forward to, and a reason to continue to dream.

Then, of course, there was Christmas itself which included traveling to both Baltimore and Lancaster on the same day. Like the party, I refused to believe I was sick and I carried on as I normally would have, more or less. The activities of the day were exhausting, but sometimes emotional well-being was more important to me than physical well-being.

All in all, my physical recovery from surgery took about a month and a half. Both surgeons were extremely pleased with the results of their respective surgeries and they both said I was doing great—much better than most who had gone through what I had. The scabs eventually healed and the scars began to fade. There were only two things about my surgery that I was still uncomfortable with. During the mastectomy, the breast cancer surgeon had to remove substantially more breast tissue than he had originally predicted. When the plastic surgeon completed the reconstruction with the latissimus dorsi flap from my back, it was not enough to completely fill the space that was left empty. The new breast sat slightly to the left of where the original breast had been, which left a hallow divot towards the center of my chest.

Secondly, the axillary dissection of lymph nodes from under my arm left that area of my arm permanently numb and slightly swollen. The surgeon warned me that there was no way to avoid it. He also warned me about lymphedema, which was severe and permanent pain and swelling under the arm that could be caused by any trauma to that arm at any time throughout the rest of my life. That meant I had to avoid all needles, blood pressure cuffs, scratches or cuts to that arm indefinitely. I would also have to avoid all saunas and hot tubs because they could cause a build-up of fluid under my arm that could not be drained or removed in any way. Though I had no signs of lymphedema throughout my recovery, it would still pose a threat for the rest of my life.

Through it all, George (still my Knight in Shining Armor) was amazing! He was most gentle, loving and patient. He slept in a most uncomfortable chair by my bed each night in the hospital. He put up with everybody's opinions of the best way for him to take care for me, and he helped me in the bathroom doing things no man should ever be asked to do. He looked at me, and even though he saw my ugly scabs, scars and mutilation, he told me I was beautiful. He told me every day that he thought I was sexy, and even though he was most anxious to make love to me, he was willing to wait as long as it took for me to be comfortable physically and emotionally. Best of all, when I was feeling sore or scared or depressed, he held me.

With three weeks of recovery behind me, I moved on to the next step in my treatment…chemotherapy. At the oncologist's office, the nurse practitioner reviewed with me all the paperwork I had completed previous to my appointment. It was the same information I had shared with the breast cancer surgeon and the plastic surgeon, but apparently they all wanted the information in their own computers. I was getting bored repeating the same answers to the same questions over and over again.

Once she completed reviewing my background information, the nurse asked me if I understood why I was there at the oncologist's office. I told her I understood I had breast cancer. I understood the surgeon removed the tumor and the infected breast tissue that surrounded it, along with what he called "clear margins" which meant he took extra tissue to be sure he got it all. I understood the cancer had spread to one lymph node under my arm which meant it was possible it had spread to other parts of my body, including my lungs, my liver or my bones. I understood I was to be treated with chemotherapy in hopes to prevent (or delay) a possible recurrence, and there was no guarantee the treatment would work. She seemed pleased that I had the right answer.

The nurse then continued to advise me of all the probable side effects I would experience from the chemotherapy, including nausea, mouth sores, loss of hair and a diminished immune system (which would leave me highly susceptible to infection), just to name a few. On the pre-appointment questionnaire, I mentioned I had had a minor toothache previous to my diagnosis. I couldn't tell if it had actually gone away or if my mind just became too preoccupied with the cancer that I could no longer feel it. The nurse informed me I would have to go to the dentist to verify there was no decay in my mouth. She said even if I had not mentioned the toothache, they were going to send me to the dentist anyway. She explained that if there was any sign of decay in my mouth, it could infect the rest of my body through those open mouth sores and could ultimately kill me.

I could not believe what I was hearing. All I could think was, "Do you mean to tell me I have mutilated my body and have endured unimaginable physical and emotional pain and now it could all be for nothing because I could end up dead if I do not subject myself to one more doctor's poking and prodding me? Have you any idea what you are asking me to do? Have you any idea what I have already been through?" I had not been to the dentist for over two years and for some reason the thought of having to go terrified me more than the surgery did.

Along with what were considered to be temporary side effects from the chemotherapy, there was one that could be permanent—infertility. She noticed I had mentioned the topic on my questionnaire and suggested that I consult with the infertility doctor again before I started my treatments. She said it might be possible to freeze my eggs or take some other preventative measures that would increase my chances of conceiving after chemo. I decided on the spot that that was not going to happen. When we had tried the two inseminations, I was so sure they were going to work. Finding out differently was devastating to me. If I subjected myself to the process of freezing my eggs just to have it not work again, I was afraid I would never be able to recover. Besides, we had already decided to leave it in God's hands, and I was not going to change my mind. Furthermore, I was not going to endure one more doctor or take the chance my frozen eggs would one day be considered useless refuse.

The nurse then went on to explain the importance of contraceptives. I was really getting angry. For three and a half years I had painstakingly recorded when I got my period each month in order to predict when I would be ovulating so that we knew when our chances would be at their highest to conceive. Now she was telling me I had to maintain my records to predict when our chances of conceiving would be at their lowest? I thought, "What else do I have to endure? What else!"

The oncologist came in and went on to explain that I was to receive a total of eight chemotherapy treatments, one every three weeks for a total of six months. The first four rounds would use a combination of drugs called Adriamycin and Cytoxan; the last four would use a drug called Taxol. Each of the drugs had their own way of destroying cancer cells and was most effective when used in combination with the others. The good news: no radiation treatments would be required.

Chapter Six

Value in "Vulnerable"

January 9, 2002 I had my first round of chemotherapy. My appointment was for 9:45am. The nurse guided George and me back to the chemo room. It was a large room with eight or nine vinyl reclining chairs lining the walls, facing the center. Off to one side of the room were two private rooms, one with a recliner chair and one with a bed, each with a little TV. I was advised at a previous visit that I could request a private room if I felt it would help ease my nerves, so that was exactly what I did. They had warned me that the private rooms might be occupied if they had patients who were very sick, so they could not guarantee either of the rooms would be available for me. I was so grateful to find the room with the recliner chair empty with a post-it note on the door that read, "Please try to reserve for Sabina." I knew I would not be able to handle watching all the other sick people sitting in the communal chairs with IV's sticking out of them. I also knew I needed a diversion to keep my mind off the reason I was there. The TV was most helpful in keeping my mind off having cancer and being injected with "medicine" that was going to make me feel sick and lose my hair.

The nurse instructed me to take a seat in the recliner and George to sit in a small chair next to me. Then she drew four tubes of blood which she took into the lab (which was right there in the chemo room) to make sure my infection fighters were strong enough to withstand the chemo drugs. She was back in about ten minutes to tell me everything looked great, and proceeded to start an IV drip of "pre-meds" which were supposed to help reduce, or at least delay, any negative side effects of the chemo. I had been advised previously that the Adriamycin and Cytoxan would most likely make me nauseous for a few days. The pre-meds prevented those effects from occurring while the drugs were being injected during my treatment, and lasted until a few hours after I got home. They dripped through the IV for about 30 minutes.

When my nurse heard the beeping of the IV machine, she came in with a tube of Adriamycin, which was pink in color, and another IV bag of clear saline. She explained she had to manually "push" the Adriamycin simultaneously with the saline through my IV tube to dilute it. It only took about ten minutes.

Lastly came the Cytoxan, which dripped through the IV for a half an hour. The nurse warned me that the Cytoxan could cause my sinuses to fill during its infusion, and if it became too much to bear, she could slow down the drip over an hour. Twenty minutes into the Cytoxan, I could feel painful pressure and a very disturbing numbness starting at the nape of my neck, crawling straight up to the top of my head. My sinuses filled and I felt like I had to sneeze. It was difficult to open my eyes and I was afraid to move. It was very uncomfortable, but all I could think about was getting out of there. Extending the visit another half hour seemed unbearable to me, so I didn't mention my discomfort until it was over. The nurse said the next time she would set it for the full hour. I didn't argue.

At 12:45pm, I was finished. The nurse sent me on my way with prescriptions for anti-nausea medicine and instructions to eat bland foods for the next several days, and I was out of there! My head cleared up about a half an hour later. George took me home then went to the pharmacy and grocery store to stock up on bland foods. I loved pound cake, which was a suggestion on the bland food list, so I ate quite a bit of that, feeling a little like I was getting away with something. I felt pretty good until 4:45 when the nausea set in. The pound cake ended up not being all I had made it out to be. The nausea was unbearable.

I wanted so desperately to make myself sick to get it over with, but the nurse warned me the chemo drugs were already going to make me dehydrated, and I was afraid that getting sick would only make me feel worse (if that was even possible). The schedule of "post-meds" I was to take did not start until the following day—apparently they thought the pre-meds would carry me through the night. I laid doubled-over on the couch for about three hours until I finally begged George to call the on-call doctor. He suggested I start the post-meds immediately, instead of waiting until the following day. I was asleep on the couch by 8:30, went to bed around midnight, and slept pretty well through the night.

I called my nurse the following day, as I promised I would, and shared with her the misery I felt the night before. She promised it would get better each round. She said because each patient reacts so differently to the chemo drugs, they did not want to prescribe any unnecessary medication until they knew how the drugs were going to affect me personally. Now that they knew just how miserable I was going to feel, they would increase my prescriptions and have me start them sooner the next time. It amazed me that the whole time the cancer was growing in me I did not feel the least bit sick, but now that the cancer had been removed and I was getting medicine, I felt sicker than I ever had.

Day Three after chemo, I experienced the worst diarrhea, cramps and hot flashes of my life. See, I had to take the chemo to fight the cancer; I had to take the post-meds to fight the nausea from the chemo; I had to take the stool softeners and drink prune juice to fight the post-meds; and now I had to take something else to fight the diarrhea from the stool softeners and prune juice. I could not understand how God could let this happen to anyone! It was too much!

That day, I became so desperate for someone to come help me. George had to work all day and my parents had just been there the night before. I tried to call my older brother in Colorado, my younger brother in State College then finally reached a good friend who said she was on her way. For the first time, I literally cried out to God for help. I was so miserable—physically, emotionally and spiritually. My heart was breaking and I was feeling totally alone. I finally got desperate enough to call the church I had stopped in after my diagnosis. There had to be a reason for lugging around that "emergency kit" all my life and I was counting on the contents to not be expired.

I was born and raised Catholic, but I hadn't really practiced since I received my Confirmation in the Eighth Grade. I knew it was the church I technically would belong to based on where I lived, but I just never got anything out of going to Mass, so I stopped making the effort. Several friends that grew up in St. Anne's with me had been by to visit through my recovery and told me they were also searching for a stronger faith and a deeper relationship with God. They began their search outside the Catholic Church, but I did not feel comfortable giving up on a faith that I never really knew anything about. I always felt at home in the Catholic Church, and I was anxious to learn more about it before giving it up.

It was a Saturday when I called the church. A man answered the phone and warned me I likely would not reach a priest in his office on a Saturday, but he'd transfer the call and I'd likely get a voicemail. God apparently was waiting for me. Father John picked up his phone. I told him my name, my history with the church, and my desperation caused by a breast cancer diagnosis. I was lost, scared, sick, maybe dying, and I had a lot of questions. He came to my home two days later. He sat with me in my living room for an hour and a half and answered all of my burning questions about being Catholic like, Why is Mass important? … Why do we have to confess sins to a priest? … What does it mean to be Catholic? … What's the difference between the Catholic Church and any other church?

I really don't remember the words he used to answer my questions, but I do remember his answers being simple, logical, non-judgmental, and ultimately satisfying to me. He was kind and patient with me. He was not at all like the men I only ever saw at the altar—reading scripture, changing bread and wine into the body and blood of Christ—appearing to me to be non-approachable, self-righteous, unforgiving, perfectly holy men of the Church who were hell-bent on pointing out to me every blessed mistake I've ever made. No, Father John was compassionate and caring and merciful, and because of him, cancer became the best thing that ever happened to me.

After all my burning questions had been satisfied, I asked Fr. John if I could follow him back to the church so that he could show me around (so I wouldn't feel so out-of-place if I came to Mass). He accepted my request. Not only did he show me where to park, what door to walk in and where the sanctuary was, but he took me into the administrative offices, introduced me to the people working there, invited me to register in the parish, and encouraged me to participate in a couple groups to meet people. He had told me: "If you feel like you don't know God, you need to spend time with people who do, because God is in people."

One group that he recommended was called WINGS (which stood for "Women IN Growth Spiritually"). It was a women's spiritual support group. He said he had heard nothing but great things about it, and he thought it would be a great place for me to start. The second group he mentioned was a class that was available to non-Catholics who were considering joining the Church (called RCIA—the Rite of Christian Initiation of Adults). The class taught the very basic fundamentals of what Catholics believe, and even though I was already Catholic, I could sit in on the class just to learn more about it. What he said about spending time with people made sense to me, so I took contact names and numbers for both groups and I called both of them later that afternoon to register. I was most excited about having places to be. I had grown so weary of looking at the same four walls of my home and lying on the couch. I was excited to get started in the groups right away, but they weren't starting for about five more weeks. I didn't think I'd ever make it that long.

Day 13 from my first round of chemo, I made an appointment with the girl who cuts my hair. I explained I had been diagnosed with breast cancer, had started chemotherapy, and wanted to have my head shaved and my wig styled before my hair started to fall out. I asked her if she would be able to handle doing that for me, even if I started to cry. She said she would be happy to do anything I needed. My appointment was scheduled late in the afternoon, which worked out well since George was working late. The stylist was very good to me. When she started to shave my head, she started in the back, so as I was looking in the mirror, I couldn't see any difference. She stopped before moving toward the front of my head and asked if I wanted to close my eyes. I said no, I wanted to feel in control. I told her I was going to cry, but just keep going; and she did.

She did not waste any time getting the wig on my head, cutting bangs into it, and shaping and layering the back and sides. Though I wasn't happy with the color (because who can pick a hair color from a wig catalog without matching it to her skin tone—especially with a pale, sickly skin tone that one acquires from chemo), but I was happier with it styled. She did not even charge me for the haircut. People like her really surprised me throughout my cancer journey, making small gestures that made such a big impact on my recovery. That evening, my parents came to take me to dinner (which soon became a ritual every Monday night). They loved the new look and thought I looked glamorous. Though I still was not excited about it, I was glad other people thought it looked nice.

It was midway through my second round of chemo when the women's spiritual support group started. They met every Tuesday morning for two hours, and that particular session was to last nine weeks. I could not wait to go! I was so hungry for a sense of spirituality, community and friendship, and I was most anxious to find it all there in the church. When I walked in, I was greeted by one of the facilitators I had spoken with on the phone. She introduced me to the leader of my table, who also happened to be a breast cancer survivor. As the other women trickled in (about fifty women total), my table leader introduced me to the other five women of our table, including yet another survivor.

Throughout my life, though I was most contented being alone, I had always been very outgoing, sociable and excited to be the center of attention when I was around other people. Breast cancer had a way, however, of making me vulnerable, quiet and reserved. Normally, in a new social situation such as this, I would have been the first to introduce myself, start a conversation, and get the meeting started. This morning, however, I sat quietly, with a timid smile on my face, taking in all the sights and sounds, waiting for conversations to be started by others. All the women at my table had already heard a little of my story and were most welcoming and friendly. They made me feel comfortable from the very beginning and I was so excited to finally be making friends.

The meeting started with a prayer, then quiet time to reflect on several scripture passages. I had never really read the bible before, and really had no idea what I was doing. I glanced at the other women and saw each of them meditating deeply in thought and writing some things in their journals. I, on the other hand, was still frantically flipping through pages, trying to find the first reading. After fifteen minutes of quiet reflection, the meeting proceeded with group discussions. What I did read from the bible I could not relate to or understand, so I remained quiet and listened to the thoughts of my group members. It amazed me how spiritual they were! I never knew Catholics to discuss their feelings about faith, and I had never experienced the mystical connection women had among each other when they shared their thoughts, beliefs and experiences. I just sat back and took it all in. When I got home that afternoon, I spent almost three hours rereading the scripture passages, and reflecting on them in my journal. I was afraid I was interpreting them wrong, but I figured God would smile on my effort anyway.

Four women from my WINGS table even came to sit with me once during one of my chemo treatments to help me pass the time. I could not believe they would go so far out of their way to comfort me and willingly come into such a dreaded place to do it! Especially the other breast cancer survivors who had lived the same hell in the same exact place a few years before. How could they ever willingly go back in there? I had only known them for two months, yet there they were—supporting me like they had known me my whole life.

It was around that time that the RCIA classes started too. Some of the topics they covered were how to pray, how to build a "personal relationship with Jesus", and what really happens at the Mass. For every question they answered, at least a dozen more came to mind. The teachers' answers were sincere and personal, and I felt like I could trust them.

The greatest lesson I learned in WINGS and RCIA was how to be *vulnerable* and *teachable*. My adult life as I knew it up to that point was about having all the answers, knowing all I needed to know to skate through life unscathed, and knowing what felt comfortable had to be right, or at least right enough for me. But cancer had a way of proving to me that there had to be more to life than that. That maybe there was value not only in being vulnerable, but also value in suffering itself. Stepping out in faith was very challenging to me. Just because I *wanted* to have faith, to know God, and to be a good Catholic, it didn't make it so.

The more I learned about God's truth, the more I feared. I feared everything! I feared having to give up the things in life that were pleasurable to me. I feared being a hypocrite—coming to Mass and still doing things God wouldn't be pleased I did. I feared knowing, loving and talking about God. What if He only spoke to me through suffering? If I admitted to wanting that relationship, would he keep me sick or make me suffer in even harder ways? I feared appearing weak for needing God in my life. I was afraid to talk about faith because I didn't want to interfere with other people's values and points of view. I was afraid to look like a fool at Mass, not knowing what to say or do, not knowing the prayer responses, not knowing the songs, not knowing when to sit, stand or kneel. I was afraid it would be so obvious I had no business being there.

Despite my fears, I registered in the parish and started going back to Mass. I didn't know what I was doing. I still didn't know the difference between the "Old Testament", "New Testament" and the "Gospels", or where to find them in the bible, or even in the book in the pew. Even if I just listened to the readings, I had no idea what they meant and I felt like I was trying to be somebody I wasn't. I listened to the priest's homily after the readings, expecting surely he would make sense out of whatever was just read, but still he spoke way over my head. Even the prayers I could recite from memory from when I was a child had no meaning to me and moved nothing in my heart.

It was uncomfortable for me to be at Mass and in WINGS and RCIA but I clung to the belief that there had to be a reason for my cancer. There had to be something more that God was calling me to. I already lived life afraid of being uncomfortable, and it wasn't getting me anywhere. If nothing else, I could feel this was a holy place and these were not perfect, but still holy, people. I knew I was where I needed to be. And although each week I questioned if I would go back, each week I just kept trusting this was where God wanted me to be, and I went back.

Little by little I started to feel more comfortable in Mass. I started to become familiar with the flow of the Mass, and to recognize the parts when I was supposed to respond. I started going early so I could find my place in the book in the pew and I read the readings before Mass would start. I started looking through my bible at home and started to become familiar with what books were in the Old Testament, the New Testament, and the Gospels. I asked questions in my classes and people were kind and patient and convincing with their responses.

I also started to pray more. One thing I learned in those classes was that writing in a journal was actually a form of prayer, and that all prayer is pleasing to God. I had started a journal when I first felt the lump in my breast. (I knew I was about to experience something that would be worth documenting.) I kept a separate section for "physical", "emotional" and "spiritual" because it was easier for me to compartmentalize my thoughts and it gave me a sense of control over what was happening to me. When I learned that what I was doing was already prayer, it gave me a little more confidence that I was doing something right.

Months into my journaling, I started to recognize God's responses to the questions and fears I was writing about. In writing things down, pen to paper, it slowed my mind down long enough for God to get a word in edgewise. What I mean is, I'd start writing something, and the next thought and entry in my journal was "maybe…". New thoughts, new ideas, new perspectives started creeping into my journal, and ultimately into my head and heart, and I started to see things differently than I ever had before.

Money, or lack thereof, soon became a struggle. We had to start using a credit card for groceries, gas and incidentals. We hadn't used a credit card since before we were married, and we were still trying to pay off what we had charged back then. It really upset me that I could not do my share of the work to make the money to pay the bills; but I knew in my heart I was doing the right thing by taking time off. Taking time for myself to get well, and becoming a better, happier, more balanced person than I was before I even got sick was more important than money.

I knew eventually I would get back to work, and eventually we would get everything paid off. I learned to give up my worries again to God, and focused on my new priorities of growing in my faith. I began to realize I would never have had the opportunity in my lifetime to take time off just for me (without having to worry about kids or anybody else), if it had not been for my diagnosis. I started to count my blessings and accepted my diagnosis as a positive way to turn my life around.

One day my Mom had called and raved about a missionary priest who was visiting at St. Anne's all week. She thought it would do me some good to hear him speak, so I took my pain medication and drove to Lancaster to meet this priest. It was the first time I had been back to the church I grew up in since my diagnosis and I received so many hugs, smiles and tears from people I barely recognized from my childhood. They had all been praying for me every week at Mass, and they were all happily surprised to see me. Seeing them all felt like I had taken some sort of vitamin that took away everything bad I was feeling and gave me the energy to get through the evening.

After the presentation, I went to the reception and met the priest. I introduced myself and explained that I had been diagnosed with breast cancer and was undergoing chemotherapy treatment. We spoke a couple minutes then he took a step back, looked deep in my eyes (seemingly to the very depth of my soul) and said, "Your calling is to minister to other women. You will use your experience to help others." I already knew that, but it made me a little weak in the knees to hear it from this Godly person who seemed to have been sent just to reassure me. In that moment, I felt no pain and I felt that some burden had been lifted from me. It was very powerful.

The following day, my Mom called to tell me how proud she and my Dad were to have me there the night before. They had watched me in awe as I greeted their friends with hugs and smiles and they were inspired by my presence. No words can describe how I felt hearing those words from my own mother. My parents are the ones who inspire and teach me. How could they possibly feel that I was an inspiration to them? It was then that I realized God had placed me in a very special and important position to be witness to

Him and to inspire others. I never considered myself to be anyone's inspiration—I was just doing what I needed to do to survive. I thought everything I was doing was really very selfish and personal. I did not anticipate anyone noticing what I was doing, let alone be inspired by it, and I almost felt guilty for receiving so much praise.

CHAPTER SEVEN

Something More

When my six months of disability was up, I officially went back to work at the cable company with two chemo treatments left to go. Physically, I felt ready to work and though I tired quickly, I believed I could perform the tasks required of me, just as I had before I left. Emotionally, however, I was a mess. As I sat down at my desk, I began to cry. I was not ready to be there. I had decided six months ago I was not going to be able to work and deal with chemo at the same time, yet there I was, at work with two more treatments to go. I was not ready to focus on the trivial things that required my attention throughout the day at work when the thought of two more treatments, physical fatigue and mental anguish over the way I looked still weighed heavily on my mind. I felt like I was being forced back in time to my "old life" after having worked so hard over the past six months to develop my "new life". I had changed so much in those six months but nothing in my work environment had changed at all. I wished I had a brand new job so I could feel I was just adding it to everything else that had become new in my life. I hated the feeling of moving backwards.

I also felt that everyone at work seemed so anxious for me to forget all about the prior six months. I did not want to forget. I was afraid to forget. I desperately did not want to go back to the way I was back then and it upset me that no one could understand that. Luckily I had found out that I still had over one hundred hours of disability pay available to me, which meant I could work partial days based on the way I was feeling. I figured out if I would work six hours each day, I would have enough disability hours to get me through the rest of my treatments, including taking three whole days off after each, so that was what I did. I settled back into work, and once my disability hours were used up, I decided to stay part-time at thirty hours a week. I felt I had much more important things to do with those extra ten hours a week than work.

My final chemo treatment was not as dramatic as I thought it would be. My normal doctor was out of the office, and even my own personal nurse who had administered all seven of my treatments to that point had taken a vacation day, so I didn't even get to say goodbye. I got over that quickly and was just elated to be walking out of that private room for the last time!

One sleepless chemo night about halfway through my eight treatments, the idea came to me to have a Cancer Kiss Off Party to thank everyone who helped me get through "Cancer World". My guest list included family, old friends, the ladies from my WINGS group, several people from work and even the doctors and nurses who took care of me. It took weeks to plan and prepare, but it finally came to be on August 3rd. I originally considered having the party at a local restaurant, but my sister-in-law, Linda so graciously offered her home instead. I attached a special thank-you note to each invitation that read: "Cancer World is officially behind me and I am ready to celebrate! For the past nine months, you, your love and your prayers uplifted me and gave me the strength to carry on. For that, I'd like to thank you by inviting you to a very special party in your honor. Cancer came into my life with a bang, and I want it to go out with a bang. If you are unable to make it, please accept this invitation as a most sincere and heartfelt thank-you. I will never forget what you've done for me."

A total of 89 people were invited, and 41 came. Though I was not expecting anyone but family, I was pleasantly surprised to see several new friends there. None of the doctors or nurses came, as I expected, but I did receive several very nice responses telling me how pleased they were to hear I was finally finished and doing so well.

It was a perfect day, complete with favors, games and prizes. The favors included sunglasses as a symbol of my bright future and I decorated Linda's house with 100 balloons that had lips printed all over them, symbolizing my cancer "kiss off". The prizes included gift baskets that I assembled out of things that had special meaning to me. In each basket I included a note that read: "To the recipient of this prize: I chose the contents of this basket because they each have special meaning to me, since my diagnosis with breast cancer, and I hope they become meaningful to you. They also symbolize my wishes for you… I kept a journal the past nine months of all my experiences and feelings and it grew into a testimony of all my blessings. I hope you use this journal to keep track of your blessings each and every day and look back every once in a while to see how blessed and loved you are. The candle is for peace and serenity. May the smell of it relax you and help you focus on all that is good in your life. The camera is for documenting memories with those you love most. Life and love are precious—make them last. The calling card is for keeping in touch with the people in your life who so desperately need to hear your voice. Who can you make smile today? Lastly, the angel is to look over you, protect you, guide you and comfort you, as you have done for me over the past nine months." That party was the perfect celebration for the ending of my cancer journey, and I was eager to look forward.

September 11th (of all days), 2002, I had another operation under the hands of my plastic surgeon to readjust the original reconstruction he performed at the time of my mastectomy. Though I would never be able to look the way I did before that first surgery, the surgeon convinced me he could make the new breast look more natural. When all was said and done, he achieved what I expected in one particular area, but overall, I was disappointed. The new breast looked a lot smaller than I anticipated. For all I had been through using the latissimus dorsi muscle from my back (the long scar below my shoulder blade, enduring two separate surgeries, and still ultimately feeling disfigured) I wondered if I would have made different choices about reconstruction.

Sometimes the nagging fear of recurrence made me question what would happen if a tumor were to grow underneath the new construction. Would my muscle that was used for the reconstruction ultimately be removed, leaving me with nothing but scars and muscle taken from my back for nothing? If I had gotten an implant, and all remained well, maybe I would have felt prettier and sexier, and if there were ever to be a recurrence, it could easily have been removed. Or maybe if I had no reconstruction at all, I would never have had to worry about it again.

Ultimately I told myself that life is entirely too short to continue questioning what could have been different, so, after healing from the second surgery, I had decided to put cancer completely behind me and move on.

I refocused my attention on living a better life and found peace in being different. I dove deeper into my search for true faith by volunteering at bingo at the church, and joining a Saturday Morning Book Group of about eight women who read a book on a particular faith topic then met each week to discuss it. I wanted to keep meeting people as Fr. John had said, and the more I learned about God, Jesus and the Church, the more interested I became.

At one point I felt the sudden need to have images of Jesus in our home. Everyone spoke about building a relationship with Him and talking to Him frequently and I knew in order to do that I would need to be able to see Him. One day I spotted in a store an image of Jesus bearing his Sacred Heart. I instantly felt connected to Him and knew that was the image I wanted in my home—in a prominent place in my home, where I could see Him (and everyone else who came to my home could see Him) all the time. I bought it and brought it home. George was at work when I got home, and I was going to be at work when he returned. I left the 12x14 framed image on the kitchen table with a note that said one day I would like this to be in a prominent place in our home, but I was willing to keep it in a closet until he was ready. When I got home that evening, it was hanging prominently in our living room (where it remains to this day).

For three more years I struggled working at the cable company. While I was desperately seeking personal and spiritual fulfillment and purpose, the company was growing more and more "corporate" with more and more emphasis on "the bottom line". I tried desperately to make the most out of my being there. I tried to make the company better, the employees better, the customers better—but I was told it was not my place to try to make anything better. I prayed for direction and for God to show me his will for my future. I was open for anything and growing more and more desperate to get out of the cut-throat cable company.

I considered writing a book and beginning a career in public speaking. In between WINGS and RCIA homework when I was sick and on disability, I had also read What Color is Your Parachute by Richard Bolles. The exercises in the book walked me through my God-given talents and the things I enjoyed doing most which was intended to help me realize what kind of work I would be most satisfied with and most successful at doing. I was still not interested in a "career", but I was desperately seeking purpose in my life and wondered where to go from there. The book and exercises helped me to realize that I had a gift and interest in teaching adults, so I tried to figure out how I could incorporate that into my life experiences and the obligation and calling I felt to use them to help other people.

In October of 2004 the director of the Cancer Center invited me to be the keynote speaker at the next Women's Breast Care Conference the following year. She said I could speak about anything I wanted, and I had a year to figure out what that might be. I could hardly wait, but at the same time, I questioned whether or not I had anything worthwhile to say. I trusted God would direct me through that year and inspire me to share something fantastic.

Writing and speaking seemed to be a logical response to the persistent question of what I should be doing with my life if I am not going to have babies, so in addition to planning my speech, I set out to write my first manuscript about my cancer experience (much of which is now part of this book). Though I never did get it published, Deacon Neil (who had taken me under his wing when I was sick) and his wife, Vicki (who was facilitating WINGS when I started) printed about five hundred copies of it and we handed it out to anyone we thought might benefit from it.

Those moments of actively trying to find purpose in my life were often mixed with some degree of depression. I wrote in my journal on July 6, 2005 after yet another month without a baby: "That's seven years, times twelve months, equals eighty-four, plus last month and this month, that makes eighty-six times God has broken my heart. Linda just had Evan, her second, a week ago. I have photo album upon photo album of my life, with no one to pass them on to. What purpose is my life? For three and a half years now I believed God took my breast, the muscle from my back, my lymph nodes under my arm, my security and my dreams, all for a purpose. I expected to be aware of that purpose by now. He, of all people, knows how I have always dreamed of being a wife and a mom. Why would he deprive me of the one thing I have always wanted? Why am I stuck working for a company who doesn't care about doing things right? I never dreamt of working at a desk on a computer for a living. I don't dream of anything anymore. I don't have dreams or aspirations or passion to do anything anymore. I don't dream of traveling because George hates to go anywhere. I don't dream of money or shopping because they only get me things—things I soon get bored with and throw away. I don't dream of speaking anymore because I don't feel passionate enough about anything to share it."

That was written just days before another follow-up mammogram. (The doctor required me to have one every six months for five years.) I would often get angry that God allowed me (and George) to suffer the monthly pain and hormonal emotions of a healthy reproductive system without the benefit of babies to come with it, and that He made me endure more mammograms on top of it!

July 9th I wrote: "I've lost hope for conceiving a baby and I have nothing in my future to strive for or dream about. Nothing to look forward to. People with children can always look forward to their next milestone—graduating, getting married and having babies of their own. They have a purpose for being here—to contribute to the replenishing of the human race. What am I if I can't contribute? Then there are other people who dream about advancing in their careers. I've never wanted a career and I most certainly don't want one now. The thought of climbing the corporate ladder cannot be farther from me. Other people strive for their own business, to be successful, to make a lot of money, to buy a lot of things. Though I love shopping and surrounding myself with new things, I love it for the change, not for the materialistic part of it. When I get new, I throw old away because I like change. I don't need to replace old with bigger and better—just different. So what else is there? What could I possibly dream about?"

I continued: "I think this is the worst I ever felt. I don't remember ever having such a bad attitude and outlook on life. But I don't know how to make it better. It's not that I'm ungrateful for all of my many, many blessings. I do realize how lucky and blessed I am. George is the perfect husband, and above all else, being a wife was always the first and primary part of my life-long dream. It should be all I need. He should be all I need. I realize my life is very easy now—that God has been granting me peace. My entire family is alive and healthy. I'm not obligated to take care of parents' finances or paperwork; no one is bed-ridden in a hospital or nursing home. I don't have to share our space with anyone. I don't have to sacrifice anything. I know this. And I am grateful. But…"

Later in that same journal entry I wrote: "Mom's advice to me would be to get involved in something, like American Cancer Society's walks and fundraisers and committees. It's weird. I don't know that I believe in raising money to find a cure for cancer. Cancer blessed me with renewed faith and it drew me closer to God. Without suffering, what opportunities would we have to love each other? This morning at Prayer Group, we talked about 'sacrificial love' and how it brings you closer to God. If our lives were nothing but what I have right now—"peace", no demands, no need for sacrifice—what would life be? Just more of what I'm feeling now—lack of direction, lack of passion, lack of dreams. … Suffering is starting to make sense to me now. In all this nothingness I've been feeling, God has just revealed to me what He wants me to say in my speech. That without suffering, we would not know the depth of His love or the depth of the love from our spouses, our family, friends or strangers (like 9/11). I've been so angry at God, but He still loves me. He loves me more than I can imagine. I am still suffering. I am still scared of a cancer recurrence. I am still angry that I can't have a baby, and I am still sad that I don't have any dreams or aspirations. But in this suffering—through this suffering, God is teaching me and using me for the purpose He has for me. It may be one speech. It may never happen again. When it's over I may feel even emptier than I do now, but this speech is what I can look forward to, at least for right now."

On July 15th I wrote: "I held onto the bulletin from last Sunday. The very last note on the very last page stated an administrative position is available in the parish office, 8:00am-4:00pm, Monday through Friday with an hour lunch. I didn't think much about it when I read it, but I held onto it anyway."

By the end of another horrible workday Wednesday, I decided it was worth checking into. I went straight over to the church after work. There were two women, each sitting at her own desk just inside the office door. It was a big, bright, beautiful, clean office with big windows, and Jesus was in the Tabernacle just down the hall. (A far cry from the old, dark, dingy, depressing cable building I was working in.) I asked if someone was available to discuss the position. They asked if I had a resume—that impossible requirement to apply for a job! I said I can get one together, but I wanted more information first.

Well, they were both leaving, so there were actually two full-time positions available. They scheduled and recorded baptisms, got certificates created, registered new parishioners, and oversaw the collection gathered over the weekends. It all sounded pretty simple, but also a lot more rewarding than cable. As soon as I got home I got on the internet to learn how to write a resume. I had never written one before.

I completed my resume that evening around 9:00 and emailed it to my parents and sister to proofread. By the next morning they had all approved of it, so I printed it out and took it straight over to the church. Fr. Louis, the pastor, was coming down the hallway and asked me what I was doing there. I told him I was applying for the office position (hoping to use him as a reference). He asked where I worked, took the resume out of my hands, skimmed it and said, "This says you have computer skills." He was on his way out, so I delivered my resume to one of the women in the office. She said she'd give it to the Parish Manager, Lou. That evening when I was volunteering at bingo, Fr. Louis came through the kitchen as we were cleaning up. He said I had stiff competition and one of the positions had already been filled. It just sounded like he was trying to let me down easy. In any case, he said Lou would be calling me.

By July 20th, I still hadn't heard anything from the church and I started to question if it was really the right place for me. It wasn't until July 26th that I received a message on my answering machine around 5:00pm from Lou. He interviewed me two days later. The more he spoke about the position, the more excited I got. The position he was interviewing me for was actually a brand new position with the two primary responsibilities of generating a census program for the parish and scheduling all the facilities. Lou said more would likely come as the position developed which was right up my alley! I thought it was a good interview and I felt pretty confident he'd offer me the position, but he said he had four more people to interview, then he would call me either way.

I got that call on July 30th and I got the job! I wrote: "God has rescued me once again! He saw how desperate I was. He saw me moving farther and farther away from Him, he heard my faint cries and he has lifted me up out of my darkness. He has gently turned me around to face Him, to start walking toward Him, with Him, and for Him. I am in awe that He loves me this much and that He chose ME! I am officially His employee! I can serve God all day every day without becoming a nun!" Lou said there were some things they needed to finalize and put together in the office before I could start, which would take five more weeks.

My official start day was a paid holiday, Labor Day Monday, two days after my thirty-fifth birthday. My first physical day working in the parish office was Tuesday,

September 6th (not quite two weeks after Hurricane Katrina. I'm not quite sure what it means that major events in my life seem to coincide with major national catastrophes, but in any case, it's a point of reference.) Very similar to the high I felt the summer I lived at the beach, and joined my Knight in Shining Armor at the altar, I was flying high because now I was working for the CHURCH! All of my troubles seemed to melt away. Though I didn't know exactly what it would be, I felt that God finally had a purpose for me, and I couldn't wait to find out how it would play out in my new job and new life direction.

About a month after starting my new job I gave my speech to about three hundred people at the Valencia Ballroom in downtown York for the Women's Breast Care Conference (sponsored by none other than my former employer, the cable company). I spoke about my experience with cancer, what I needed most from my family, and what value I eventually found in my suffering. The audience was very receptive and I thoroughly enjoyed sharing my story (and free copies of my manuscript) and touching other people's lives. I wondered if I'd be given any other opportunities like that to use my suffering for someone else's benefit, and my heart was soaring with the possibilities.

CHAPTER EIGHT

Receptivity and Grace

With a new hope for purpose in my life with this new position in God's Church, I continued to long for more truth and still a deeper faith. Vicki invited me to a new video program she was offering out of her home called "Women of Grace". The program consisted of reading a book by Johnette Benkovic called *Full of Grace*, answering questions in the accompanying workbook, and attending weekly meetings to watch Johnette on video and share in small groups discussions about what we were getting out of it all. I had grown to trust Vicki and other holy women of the church through WINGS and I couldn't refuse her invitation. It was an opportunity to return to that vulnerable and teachable state that proved to be so beneficial to me in the beginning. I was nervous not knowing what to expect, but still so eager to find out what God wanted to reveal to me at that point in my journey.

Through Johnette's Women of Grace program I learned about "authentic femininity", "spiritual motherhood" and "birthing Christ into the world, like His mother, Mary", which are, to this day, some of the greatest lessons I've learned so far on my faith journey. Johnette taught me that authentic femininity does not come from physically bearing children or having a beautiful body. It is, rather, a God-given vocation to nurture, to be receptive, to surrender and to trust. She explained that all women are created to be "spiritual mothers" who nurture, protect, encourage and pray for those that God puts in our path to love. And, just as the Blessed Mother birthed Jesus Christ into the world, all women are endowed with the great gift and responsibility to bear Christ into the lives of others.

Wow! God's timing was actually spot-on this time in my life! I desperately needed to hear those things, and now I was working at the perfect place to practice them all—the Church! These new lessons, revelations and perspective didn't take away my longing for true motherhood, but it definitely gave me purpose and hope that in some way, maybe God would still somehow satisfy all my deepest desires.

By the end of the Women of Grace program series, I was struggling very much with my weight. Food was a constant comfort to me over the past several years through all of my trials, and I felt that it was the one thing in my life that I could control. I suppose I was subconsciously trying to fill that interior void that I feared would never be filled by carrying a baby. I never was one to try dieting (heaven forbid I make any unnecessary sacrifices having already been forced to sacrifice so much) and I knew it would take something different—something spiritual—to change my eating habits.

At the last Women of Grace meeting at Vicki's someone mentioned they heard of a program called "The Light Weigh" which was a Catholic spiritual weight-loss program created by another woman with a video program, Suzanne Fowler. It was mentioned in the group that if anyone would consider facilitating it, others would be interested in participating. Born a leader at heart that doesn't sit around and wait for others to act, I contacted The Light Weigh the next day and within a week, all the program materials were delivered to my doorstep. I followed the official program recommendations for starting a new group and advertized The Light Weigh sessions (to be offered out of my own home) in the church bulletin. About a dozen women responded, and before long, they were all in my home sitting around my TV, listening with me to the great weight-loss and spiritual revelations Suzanne had to offer.

For many women in the group, the Light Weigh program was just another diet that was doomed to fail. For me (the goody-two-shoes rule follower that I am), it was God's answer to my plea to help me lose weight and feel better about my body image. Though I didn't need to look and feel pretty to be "authentically" feminine, I still needed to do something to feel good about myself and feel good about being a woman, even though I had only one breast and no children to show for it. The program followed a strict set of instructions including writing in the accompanying workbook every day. This was the downfall for many—not everyone loved to record their daily life in writing like I did—but it proved to be the only way this particular weight-loss program would work.

In Suzanne's first video, I heard for the first time in my life that God purposely created each one of us with a "hole in our heart" so that we would go to Him to fill it. We all make the mistake of turning to food, alcohol, shopping, new homes, new relationships, new jobs or anything else we can control, to fill the void that God created to be filled by Him alone. St. Augustine's popular quote "My heart is restless until it finds its rest in Thee" makes this "heart hole" idea make sense. We all feel dissatisfied in this life—empty and restless—because God's plan is, after testing us in fire, to satisfy our every need and desire in Heaven.

This was another great "a-ha" moment for me. It gave me some sense of security knowing that God was not only *aware* of the emptiness and restlessness I was feeling in my life—He actually placed it there on *purpose*, and *for* some great purpose. I was beginning to accept that that great purpose may have been for nothing else but to draw me closer to Him, and in a sense, I started to feel a little bit okay with that.

In each weekly video of The Light Weigh, Suzanne introduced a different saint or nugget in the "gold mine" of the Church, all the while teaching us about St. Therese of Lisieux's "little way" of sacrificing. It wasn't really St. Therese's way, but Christ's way, called redemptive sacrifice. Jesus proved that suffering and sacrifice have value when we do it for love of others—the way He did by accepting death on a cross to save us from our sins. "Through His stripes we were healed," Isaiah said.

The premise of The Light Weigh was to make food sacrifices with the prayerful intention that someone else would benefit from our little "self mortifications", whether they be a second helping, an extra cookie, or even the last bite of food on our plate. Carrying someone else's burden proved to be much easier than carrying my own, which made losing weight myself a gift to all those I sacrificed for along the way. The program worked the way it was intended to for me (because I followed all the rules and instructions) and I lost thirty pounds. I never felt prettier or more comfortable in my own skin than I did when I lost all that weight!

Unfortunately, the program did not prepare me with the humility and trust in God that I would need each time a well-meaning person complimented me on my weight loss, or a not-so-well-meaning person made a sexual comment or pass at me that would cause the fear I felt in the beach shop more than fifteen years earlier to resurface in my mind. So again, I reverted back to protecting myself by putting the weight back on and being comforted by food that made me feel safe both physically and emotionally. Still, the spiritual lessons that stuck with me from The Light Weigh have made a huge difference in my outlook on life, on suffering, and even on death, and it was one of the greatest stepping stones on my faith journey to date.

The next stepping stone was to re-visit the RCIA. Recalling my *Parachute* lesson for finding fulfillment in my job and therefore ultimately finding fulfillment in my life, I realized becoming an RCIA catechist (teacher) would be a great way to honor God with the gifts he'd given me—my life experiences, as well as a knack for using them to teach and inspire others. Convincing Sister Jean, the Director of

Religious Education, that I was qualified, eager and ready to teach the depth of truth that is protected by the Church, however, took some doing. Instead of putting me directly on the teaching team, Sister Jean encouraged me to participate in class another year—this time as a sponsor to a candidate interested in receiving her sacraments, Rachel (who later became my goddaughter).

I was disappointed at first, and felt that I was being held back from fulfilling my destiny to be a teacher, but Sister Jean's wisdom soon became evident. I started to realize that just because I heard something before didn't mean I "got it" or understood it to the extent that God intended to reveal it to me and it often took class discussion to make things sink in. Supporting Rachel on her own journey also gave me a different perspective on the subject matter of the classes and it gave me a certain responsibility to understand the lessons more deeply and more personally. It soon became evident just how much more I had to learn before I could effectively teach, and I became ultimately grateful for this delay to my life-fulfilling destiny.

RCIA, unlike all the other groups I was participating in, focused primarily on the theology, history and authority of the Church. The weekly lessons explained why the Church believes and teaches what she does on so many different topics like the sacraments, the dignity of human life, the "real Presence in the Eucharist", and Mary. Converting the cold, hard, seemingly antiquated and unrelatable truth of the Church into an internalized and personal experience of faith in my own heart took time and grace and effort—an effort I was most eager to make.

The following year, likely with some trepidation, Sister Jean included me on the teaching rotation and gave me a few topics to study, prepare and facilitate on my own (though the more knowledgeable and experienced team members were close at hand to fill in the blanks and answer questions I wasn't prepared for). It's true that the best way to learn is to teach. As a member of the teaching team, I was given multiple resources to research my assigned topics, and I dug deep to find ways to relate them to my personal life. It was in that true study of the faith that I found the truth that I could relate to, understand and believe, and it started to become MY faith, MY truth, MY theology, history and authority, and MY honor and responsibility to share it.

The greatest lesson I learned as a participant and a member of the RCIA teaching team was The Story of Salvation History. It was through "The Story" that Jesus became a real person in my life who I came to know, care about, and have a real relationship with. Just as I came to know and fall in love with George, I came to know and fall in love with Jesus. I started talking to Him. I started putting pictures of Him around my home. I started to ask His opinion on things, rely on His strength and protection, and cry on His shoulder. I started spending more time alone with Him and I started to trust Him. I came to know Him by actually reading about His story. It's all right there in Scripture and in the Tradition of the Church, and it ended up being easy to find!

Though Jesus was revealed to humanity in a particular time and space in history, He existed with God the Father (and the Holy Spirit) from the beginning, before all time. God (His Father) sent Jesus to reveal Himself (the Father) to us, to share in our humanity so that we could share in his divinity, and to show us "the Way, the Truth, and the Life". Jesus tells us the only way to know the Father is to know him, the Son, and by knowing them both, we come to love them as real Persons in our life. Jesus' mission on earth was (and continues to be) as priest, prophet, and king—a *priest* to sanctify us and unite us to the Father, a *prophet* to correct us and teach us truth, and a *king* to rule, govern and protect us.

To know Jesus, I not only needed to understand this divine nature of his, but I needed to know Him in his humanity as well. In his humanity, he had a family, a family history, family stories told from generation to generation, and a culture in which his family lived. To know Jesus, I had to get to know his family and his culture. That culture was an ancient Jewish culture. Those stories add up to "The Story of Salvation History" otherwise known as "His-Story" (which I found in the Books of Genesis, Exodus, Numbers, Joshua, Judges, 1 Samuel, 2 Samuel, 1 Kings, 2 Kings, Ezra, Nehemiah, 1 Maccabees, Gospel of Luke, Acts.) When I first read The Story, it was not as daunting as I thought it would be. It was actually surprisingly entertaining—full of drama, intrigue, horror and romance!

When the story reached Jesus' life, death and resurrection, it revealed to me how he fulfills and completes each and every anticipated promise of the Old Testament (given by God to his people). Most especially, Jesus revealed himself as the "Lamb of God"—the sacrifice made to God for the forgiveness of my sins. Reading "The Story" made Him much more than just my Savior and Redeemer—it made me see Him as the fulfillment of thousands of years of stories, promises and hopes, not only to the ancient Jews, but to me today, in this time and place.

I learned that Jesus is human in every way but sin. He knows pain. He knows about suffering. He knows how it feels to have a broken heart. He knows well the feelings of abandonment, loneliness, and what it feels like to be bullied. He knows about hunger, homelessness, and having to bear with ignorant and annoying people. He knows the love of a mother, the companionship of a best friend, and the longing to love and be loved. He knows *everything* there is to know about me, and still loves me just the same. He longs to be with me, and he longs for me to want to be with

Him. Jesus promised he will be with me until the end of time. That means He's with me now—right here—in this time and place, and in every circumstance of my life! He is the Light of the World and He sees into every dark corner of my hardened heart and comes to bring me hope, healing, joy and peace. Jesus is mercy and all that is good. Amidst all my attachments, sins, disordered desires and weaknesses, He still shows His mercy and His love for me.

The joy and exhilaration I felt after each lesson I taught in RCIA was truly a high for me, and I longed more and more for the opportunity to study, internalize and share what finally became my source of fulfillment. The participants in the class became my "spiritual children" and I started to understand Johnette's lessons on spiritual motherhood and "birthing Christ" into the world.

That's far from saying my new life in Christ was easy. With every new a-ha epiphany came more challenges to my interior spiritual life. There was a constant battle in my heart and head between right and wrong, between trusting God and staying in my comfort zone, and loving people where they were and challenging them to be better.

The two most influential people in my life are my Mom and George. Mom was the one who chose to baptize me and raise me in the Catholic Church; but she was also the one who began to see me as the over-the-top "Jesus freak" of the family. Though she goes to Mass every Sunday and volunteers in the Church, she won't let herself be "vulnerable" and "teachable" ever again. The Church has grown exponentially in wisdom and enlightenment since she was a child in Catholic school, and much is available now to teach us how to understand the unchanging truths of our faith, but my Mom still has no interest in relinquishing her "freedom to choose" what she wants to believe. Though she detests "rules", she trusts and obeys them because they are compatible with her comfort zone. They are the rules her mom taught her, and when her mom died at an early age, they are somehow what makes her feel connected to the one person who meant the very most to her. The rules are all she's ever known about the Church, and I wonder if sometimes she fears the idea of ever knowing more about the Faith than her mom did, so she refuses to learn any more. God love my mom!

This is particularly challenging to me—an adult child who will still do anything to please her, to win her love by being just what she wants me to be—nothing more and nothing less. So, it seems the more I grow in my faith and in my relationship with Jesus, the more my Mom fears me and any discussion with me about our faith. I have never doubted my Mom's love for me, but I continue to see more and more that she has her own wounds and brokenness, and she tries her hardest, just like the rest of us, to get through this life with the least amount of pain and discomfort as possible. It just hurts me so much that I could be a source of any of that pain or discomfort.

Then there's my George. He has been my protector from the first day I met him. He has fought for my love and trust and has yielded to me in innumerable ways just to make me happy. He is truly what God must have had in mind when he created husbands. He loves me, he loves his family, and he loves my family. Still, his faith journey has not yet begun. He still keeps his "emergency kit" on reserve. He is still where I used to be—satisfied with life just as it is, with no real need for God. Though he rejects all notions of fear, he is not interested in stepping out of his comfort zone. And I certainly cannot fault him for that.

When I got sick and I felt the need to call the Church, I asked George if he'd be okay with that. He didn't marry a woman who gave any priority in her life to God, and I was concerned the changes in me would change his love for me. He told me to do whatever makes me happy (it is truly his main goal in life to see to it that I am happy, God bless him), but not to expect him to need or want the same things for himself. We agreed that I would not push him and he would not hold me back. I know the seed of faith has been planted in George's heart. He reveres God, Jesus and Mary, and he loves me. Trusting in Jesus that he will touch George in his own due time, this remains to be enough for me.

That's not to say I don't still have fears. I still struggle in trusting God that he will keep our marriage happy and healthy. George has admitted to me more than once that he fears that one day I will see him as being "not good enough" for me since he does not have a spiritual life like I do. I fear that he will really believe that one day and will leave me "for my own good". So I still have to make the conscious choice to trust God, and trust my George. It's a very real fear and it takes very real practice in my heart and in my head to trust. Still, after all these years of learning and practicing faith and literally growing in my relationship with Jesus, trust does not come easily. It's one thing to trust Him to love me, protect me and feed me—it's something different to trust Him in my relationships with the people who mean the very most to me. That's why reading the bible is so necessary for me. It's there where Jesus tells me over and over again: "Be not afraid. In all things, *trust me*, and *be not afraid*."

Chapter Nine
A New Hope

The day before Thanksgiving 2010 we celebrated the upcoming holiday in the church office with pastries and mimosas (orange juice and champagne). Yes—at work, in the parish office, mid-morning—because the office was closing at noon. It was that kind of job. We worked together, prayed together, grumbled together, and yes—celebrated together. We were more like a family than colleagues—including the priests, Lou the Manager, and all of the church office and pastoral staff. I knew it was a great decision to leave the corporate world of cable and work for the Church! I loved my job!

By that evening, I started feeling a dull pain that grabbed me every once in a while with an intensity that took my breath away. I assumed it had something to do with my poor choice in diet and it would pass. The following morning, while watching our traditional Macy's Parade, I was still very uncomfortable; but later that afternoon I managed to eat Thanksgiving Dinner just fine, and when I laid my head down on my pillow at the end of the day I was able to easily drift off to sleep. By 2:30 in the morning, though, the pain was again so intense it jolted me from my sleep.

Perpetually unwilling to sacrifice my all-important traditions, though I could hardly stand up straight I still drove to the diner at the mall in Lancaster to meet my family for breakfast and do our annual Black Friday Christmas dress shopping. While we waited in line for a table at the diner, it felt like my legs were going to give out from under me. When Mom asked why I was so quiet, I told her how much pain I was in. (She always did say that if you share things that are good they're twice as good and when you share things that are bad they're only half as bad, so I never was very good at suffering in silence.) She said my symptoms sounded a lot like the ones she had when she had an appendicitis, and the scar on her belly was in the exact spot I was feeling the leg-weakening, posture-effecting pain. After finishing breakfast and buying our dresses, I quickly took my leave and headed home.

The pain was getting worse, so I consulted with the ever-faithful, all-knowing website "WebMD". I looked up "appendix". The diagram alone made me believe Mom might be right. The website said the pain from an infected appendix could be severe or just an overall feeling of not feeling well. The website also said to "trust your instincts". Well, "my instincts" always fooled me into believing that all signs of pain meant the cancer was back. I hated the idea of crying wolf for something that could end up being nothing but gas pains, but the website indicated an infected appendix was nothing to fool around with. It also said the only way to cure an infected appendix was to remove it surgically. The following day was going to be the ninth anniversary of my mastectomy and reconstruction surgery. I was so not interested in the CT scans, pelvic exams and surgery the website spoke about, but I was sure an infectious "burst" would be much worse than all of that.

It was Friday (of course), and George was working, but I was so scared by then I couldn't help but call him and ask him for his opinion on what I should do. He suggested I call the family doctor first, which I did, and got an appointment for 4:00 that afternoon. (Oh how I dread doctors' appointments late Friday afternoons!) In the meantime, I was instructed not to eat anything in case emergency tests would be needed that required an empty digestive system. This pain was not fitting into my plans for cleaning and decorating my house for our annual Christmas party just two weeks away!

George left work early to go to the doctor's with me and soon thereafter we were in the emergency room at the hospital. Seven hours, a CT scan, an ultrasound and other tests later, I was released with no known cause for my pain. (Sometimes that's worse than getting a terrible diagnosis. There had to be a cause for my pain!) Before leaving the ER, however, I was told the CT scan had revealed something—something interesting. Though it did not relate at all to the symptoms I was having the past few days, they found a large fibroid cyst in my uterus. The intern doctor in the ER told me that the fibroid likely had a lot to do with my infertility, but I would have to consult with an OBGYN about that.

Even with my medical history, I had never in my adult life acquired a regular OBGYN. I felt that my body was poked and prodded, scanned and evaluated enough for a lifetime. Since the cancer was something I could feel and ultimately be cured from, I believed God would simply let me know if I was ever in danger again. I accepted these new CT scan results as His "letting me know".

That Saturday night, I was still in a lot of pain—to the point it was causing me to have an anxiety attack. Everyone seemed to think it was "just gas", and I would just have to wait it out, but this was now four days that I had this debilitating pain and it was wearing on my emotions. To distract me from my pain, my mother-in-law told me about a story she saw on TV that morning about a woman who had a uterine fibroid surgically removed and had twins at age thirty-nine. I was forty at the time, but it still gave me much hope. God can do all things! Anything is possible!

Monday morning I felt no better, but I felt obligated to go to work. By 9:00 I was in so much pain I didn't know what to do. I went home and remembered the doctor in the ER dismissed me with instructions to follow-up with my family doctor "on Monday". When I called my family doctor for an appointment, I was told they don't do hospital follow-ups on Mondays, and, based on something they read on my file in the computer, I was to go back to the hospital. I wrestled terribly with those instructions. Why go back to the hospital? They never found the cause for my pain. What other tests could they do?

George was scheduled to work until 5:00. He couldn't just keep leaving—especially just to sit around with me and do nothing for hours while I continued to be poked, prodded and scanned. I didn't want to go back to the hospital. That bed in the ER was terribly uncomfortable and the morphine they gave me didn't ease my pain any more than ibuprofen did. I didn't think it was an emergency at that point since my symptoms hadn't changed since Friday. And honestly, I didn't trust doctors. It seemed to me that all doctors heard was that I was in pain and they would stop at nothing to get all the answers—regardless of my pain, discomfort, fears, emotions, and the thousands of dollars in bills.

The world seemed to me to be overanxious to "fix" suffering. I wrote in my journal: "This is suffering. Jesus Christ and all the saints have suffered. I am in good company. What do I do Lord? Please give me the gifts of wisdom and discernment. Please give me humility, patience, obedience, courage and strength. Please tell me what to do. Right now it is completely in my hands. I am, at the moment, totally in control of what happens to me—whether I go to the hospital or not. Jesus, I surrender the control to you. Please tell me what to do. I will obey you."

I called George again. He wasn't at all interested in revisiting the ER either. He and Mom were still convinced it was just gas, and they agreed with me that my current symptoms didn't seem "urgent", so I decided to stick it out a few more days. Though I never received any lightening strikes of discernment or revelations from God or explanations for my pain, I managed to survive five more uncomfortable days, avoid the hospital, and prepare for our Christmas party. And the pain went away.

Now prioritizing all things based on trust in God and His will for my life, I constantly watched for signs of His direction and tried to keep an open mind with courage and humility (while still trying to maintain some sort of "logic" to His promptings). I wondered if God, in trying to give me answers and ultimately a cure for my infertility, allowed the un-diagnosable gas pains to get me to the ER to get the CT scan to reveal this obvious hindrance to getting pregnant so I could get it taken care of and ultimately have babies! Could it possibly be that simple and that obvious? Well, yes, I told myself—God is simple…and obvious!

Having worked at that point five years in the parish office surrounded by holy Catholic women, I eagerly sought their advice about which doctor to see and I was easily convinced it would be worth the 40-minute drive north to the Women's Center at the closest Catholic hospital. I had grown to distrust local doctors with their emphasis on contraception and "protecting the mother" in life-threatening situations and it gave me great peace to find a doctor with the same values I had regarding human dignity—the dignity of a woman's body and the dignity of the life she carries in her womb (hoping against hope there would be a need for such a concern).

I considered what plan God might have for a baby of mine. Maybe my child would be a saint that would lead millions of people to God. I couldn't let fear keep me from allowing God to use me in His plan! I thought, "If the Blessed Mother could give birth to the Son of God with nobody in the world to help her but her husband—no hospitals, no doctors, no sanitation—nothing at all but faith—then I can endure some tests and procedures by a Catholic OBGYN in the twenty-first century."

Our first appointment was December 8th. When I walked in the door I was greeted by a crucifix hanging on the wall and I immediately felt safe and confident that I was doing God's will. Out of five doctors in that Catholic practice, the doctor that greeted us was the only one that wasn't Catholic. My heart sank a little, but he assured me he "works well with the Catholics." He was very nice, very patient, very informative, very relaxed, and very humble.

After talking with him about forty-five minutes he told us we'd be in better hands with his Catholic colleague, Dr. D who was younger and highly skilled in infertility—in particular with the new Napro Technology (that I kept advertizing recently in our parish bulletin but knew nothing about)—which this doctor admitted he was not. He said he wasn't even going to examine me because Dr. D would want to do that himself since he would be taking over my care. I appreciated that so much! It was the first time a doctor seemed to put my emotional wellbeing before his own curiosity.

This doctor said he would fill Dr. D in on our conversation and mentioned we were a "special case". I kind of liked being a "special case" because they seem to intrigue doctors the most and demand extra attention and care. I was impressed that he heard us out without rushing us, recognized our need for healing was much more complicated than a routine surgical procedure, and then still willingly stepped aside to refer us to a colleague who was more qualified to meet our needs.

Before we left, he said the fibroid in my uterus had about doubled in size in a year, which meant Dr. D would likely want to have it removed. (I was already prepared for that.) He said 8.8 centimeters wasn't huge for a fibroid—twenty to thirty centimeters would be huge (and can make women look pregnant). He said most often when fibroids are removed patients opt to remove the entire uterus. Being sensitive to the fact that that was not a consideration for me, he assured me fibroids can, however, be removed while still preserving the uterus, which was one of Dr. D's specialties. He said there was about one percent chance the fibroid could have cancer, but he said that kind of cancer is not at all relative to breast cancer and he was quite certain it was not even of any concern. As we drove away from that appointment, I really felt like we were in the right place. I really felt that God wanted me there, in that place, at that time, with Dr. D as my assigned physician. For the first time in a long time, I felt hopeful.

Dr. D was not available to meet with us until January 26th. Due to the hustle and bustle of the holidays, being busy at work and teaching RCIA classes, I was at peace with the long wait. I dreamt the night before our appointment that I was pregnant. In my dream, I was at peace and I felt happy—but that peace didn't last long. As we drove to the

Women's Center, though I felt confident that this doctor would have the ability to cure us from our infertility and help us in a morally Catholic Christian way to have babies, I was anxious.

Meeting Dr. D went as expected, and by the time we left the appointment I had an order for another MRI (and a prescription for anti-anxiety medicine to get me through it), and instructions to start paying attention to the physical signs my body gave me in regards to my fertility cycle (specifically the characteristics of any apparent vaginal mucus from day to day). My instructions included charting these bodily signs for three to four months, getting monthly blood tests to mark hormone levels at different times of my fertility cycle, then meeting again with Dr. D to review the findings.

Within the week we were at an introductory lesson on how to recognize my bodily signs of fertility and record them on a special chart. In the Church the system is called "Natural Family Planning" and it was proven to be highly effective. The facilitator said that 98% of fertile women wanting to get pregnant did so within six months of using this charting method, but I wondered how fertile could we be if we were still childless after twelve and a half years of trying to get pregnant?

The basis of the program was to increase communication between the husband and wife about their sexuality and fertility. George could not have been any less interested in such conversations. He never was a planner or deep thinker, and this was far too detailed, uninteresting, and quite honestly a little bit "gross" to talk about. He just wanted to know when and where he had to be to provide his "loving embrace" so that we could make babies. I didn't blame him. I wasn't terribly interested in all the mechanics either. If God really wanted us to have babies, He could have easily made it so at any moment without so much attention on my fertility cycle. I think I resented the whole process from the very beginning, but if this truly was God's will, I couldn't simply ignore it or say I wasn't going to give it my best effort. I relied on my rule-following "good-girl" outlook on life and did what I was told.

Ultimately, Dr. D agreed it was best to surgically remove the fibroid. During the surgery (on April 27, 2011) he found an additional probable cause for our fertility problems—"extensive" endometriosis (essentially, that's scar tissue within and around the uterus that can prevent a fertilized egg from implanting and growing in the uterus). He removed all the endometriosis he could find, along with the TWO fibroids (another smaller fibroid was hidden behind the known large one) and another cyst on my ovary, and we felt confident this was going to make all the difference.

I truly believed God had answered my prayers and that He had finally healed me!

At my surgical follow-up appointment at the Women's Center two weeks later, I was given a prescription for pre-natal vitamins and was instructed to start taking them right away. Though at least four months of vitamins would be optimal, we wouldn't necessarily have to wait that long to start trying to conceive. We only had to wait now for me to heal from surgery (which would take about eight weeks). At that appointment, I was also given the results from the blood tests I had taken the past several months. They indicated my progesterone level was low. My highest count was eight—optimal was fifteen to twenty-five. (The last time we saw a doctor about infertility I was told I had low estrogen. This time it was low progesterone.)

After about eight weeks of healing from surgery, we were given the "go-ahead" to try to conceive. We were so excited! To think, within a couple weeks we could be told we were pregnant! Along with that "go-ahead", I was told I would need to inject myself with a needle every month for four days straight at the beginning of my cycle to increase my progesterone level. I panicked. I knew I would not be able to do that, and I knew George and Mom would be too squeamish and concerned about hurting me to do it either. Thankfully our parish had an adjacent school, and though school was out for the summer, the school nurse lived nearby and was willing to administer the shots for me. Dr. D said we'd only try it for six months—if it wasn't working by then, it wasn't going to work. In my heart, though, I knew if it didn't work in the first two months, it wasn't going to work because my emotions wouldn't be able to take it any longer than that.

The deadline I gave God to tell me we weren't pregnant after that first attempted month after surgery was July 16th. Being rejected any time beyond that point in my mind would be nothing but cruel. As that date was approaching though, we were already completely convinced we were pregnant. Our whole lives and all of our waiting and suffering were coming down to this month—this month in particular. We chose baby names and discussed how we would tell our families. We made plans for a nursery and talked about work and income and how different our lives were about to become. A friend of mine at the church bought a baby necklace with a cross pendant on it that was intended for our baby to wear at "her" baptism. Deacon Neil even blessed it. George and I were both all in and never more ready to be parents!

I had a different sensation in my belly those days, like nothing I had ever felt before. I begged God not to allow me any false hope. If it wasn't so—if I wasn't pregnant—I just desperately needed Him to tell me so my hopes wouldn't go beyond where they already were. Getting my period on time would've been disappointing enough, but to be "late" and be told we weren't going to have a baby would be much too much for me to bear. I had thirteen years of disappointment—there was no room in my faith for any more. On July 15th we were at a wedding reception slow dancing and I was utterly convinced this was it—we were going to have a baby!

Then God answered. By the morning of my pointless deadline, God said, "Not yet." I was beyond devastated. How can this possibly be? How could God have let me believe for five whole days that all of our dreams were coming true? How could He let me believe that all those years of waiting to get married, all the early infertility treatments, cancer, body-mutilating surgeries, charting and injections were going to be worth it? What kind of God would do that? No God could be "loving" and let us suffer and hope and trust and believe so much in His providential timing just to, in the end, tell us we weren't fit or good enough or prepared enough to be parents!

That was it. All those years of faith and hope and trust were completely wiped out in a single moment of truth—the truth that I wasn't going to have a baby. I wrote in my journal: "Where are you?!! Jesus was in the desert for forty days. We've been here for thirteen years, waiting for a baby. I understand the cross. Was I not already embracing the cross of infertility? Was I not already pouring my heart into your Church and into my job? I *accepted* the cross ten years ago. Why wait all this time to literally nail me to it? I would have carried it into eternity for you. I would have. I was prepared. Is there still—now, in this unbearable pain and desperation of being stripped of all faith and goodness that I had in me—a possibility that there could be a resurrection for me—me and my George? How much can my George possibly bear Lord? He watched me die once already through cancer, surgery and chemo. He's carried the weight of my cross of infertility over and over and over again. How will he ever surrender and trust in you? I'm tired of praying. I'm tired of hoping. I'm tired of waiting. What is left for us? Do you really not see us? Do you really not love us?? My God, my God, why have you forsaken me? Why have you forsaken me and my George?"

I couldn't pray. I couldn't look at Jesus or Mary and say one word—just cry and bitterly walk away. I couldn't journal or go to Mass and I had a terrible time going to work. This was the last straw. I couldn't trust a God who could be so cruel. Why couldn't He just tell me a couple days sooner! I couldn't understand that. What's two days to the Creator of Time? Would it not have been worth it to Him to protect my faith in Him by giving me those two days? I was lost. More lost than I had ever been in my life. I had nowhere to go from there. No hope, no faith, no trust, no purpose, and not even a Father or Brother or Mother to talk to about it. I was beyond bitter and beyond despair.

Jesus did not let me stay in that state long. I soon realized that He said he would be with me until the end of time. He felt abandoned too, so if nothing else, I still had that connection to Him. But I questioned how I could talk to Jesus if I had no belief that the Father loved me. Jesus is one with the Father.

Hell is the absence of God and that was exactly where I was. I kept hearing the Apostle Peter's voice in my head, "Where else can we go?" There was nowhere else to go. There is no life without God. I wondered, if God would still allow us to have a baby the next month or the month after that, would I be able to forget how rejected and abandoned He made me feel in that moment? Would I ever be able to trust Him again? I just couldn't see how abandoning me and shattering my heart and faith could glorify God in the end. Isn't that the whole point to our existence—to love and glorify Him? I was already there! Why even tell me about the fibroid and endometriosis? I had already surrendered. I had already accepted my cross. I couldn't understand.

At one point I asked George if he still believed God loved us. Much to my surprise, he said, "Yes." I asked why he believed it and he said, "Because we still have so much. We still have each other and our health and the ability to try again." I was still angry and hurt, but I knew I had to make a conscious choice between believing that either God loved me or He didn't. I thought it through and realized there was no purpose to life, no hope in a future to believe that God didn't love me. By sheer process of elimination that meant He simply had to love me. I couldn't make sense of the way He was proving that to me, but I had to believe in the deepest foundation of my soul that He had to love me. I wouldn't even exist if He didn't.

With that, I decided to leave all that disappointment and rejection where it was, and move on. It was all I could do, really. Though I felt empowered in that decision, it really didn't come from any place of great faith or virtue, but more from a place of self-preservation. Either way, I was moving forward.

CHAPTER TEN

Wounds Heal

I continued to follow Dr. D's care and continued charting until the end of November 2011. That was enough. We were forty-one, and the simple fact still remained—if God wanted us to have a baby, He could give us one at any time, without all the extra added stress, anxiety, emotion and cost of fertility treatments. I surrendered my life-long desire to my God once again, and I simply left it at that.

People ask me all the time if we've ever considered adoption. Almost everyone tells me they know or have heard of a couple who struggled for years to have a baby, then adopted, then conceived on their own. There are two major reasons why adoption is not a consideration for me.

First, if adoption is considered as a "fix" to suffering or some sort of deceptive trick or deal to make with God in order to have things our own way and against His will, it is not of God. Adoption is not intended to be a default plan for people who cannot conceive a child but still long to be parents. Adoption is holy and good only when it is in accord with the will of God. I have enough difficulty discerning His will in my own life, so I certainly have no intention to discern his will for other people's lives, but I do know well how Satan, the Fallen Bearer of Light, masks evil in things that *appear good* and twists God's love and truth to suit our own agendas. For me, I know in my heart that if George and I attempted to adopt, it would be an attempt to suit my own agenda, and I know without doubt that that simply is not of God.

The second reason adoption is not a consideration for me (even if Satan could convince me that my intentions to love would be good enough reason to reject the will of God) is that I know I cannot bear any more rejection. Just because couples decide they want to adopt, it does not necessarily make it so. Most of the adoption process relies on the decisions of other people, and of course the will of God, and there are no guarantees. I cannot risk losing my faith again over any more rejection. Part of practicing virtue is knowing our limitations and I know when it comes to rejection I have reached my limit.

When the faith-shaking question of why God permits suffering surfaced again with a hernia diagnosis and yet another surgery, I took it to the cross of Jesus. I can't completely wrap my mind around it or explain it in words, but if God could allow His only begotten Son—who He loved more perfectly than I could ever begin to comprehend—to be stripped naked, whipped, spit on, humiliated and crucified on a cross, there must be value in it all. God is always in control. He reveals his strength through my weakness. He permits sin and grief and suffering and pain, but He always brings from it a greater good for those who love Him. And though I struggle all the time to understand His ways, I do love Him. And I trust He will make good of all things.

Once again with no direction or grand agenda or goal for my life, I turned my attention to the one thing that gave me purpose—my work in the church office. At that time I had been working for the church for six years. (A record for me!) The woman who had filled that first available position in the office just before me, Donna, ended up being my partner and good friend for three years. How could we not grow close with our permanently mounted desks and computers directly facing each other? We literally sat face to face for six hours a day, five days a week. Her primary responsibilities were registering new families in the parish, keeping track of memberships and address changes, and scheduling and recording baptisms. Mine, as Lou promised, continued to grow and change to include multiple large projects like a parish-wide census and a capital campaign to raise funds to renovate our parish school. That was in addition to my regular responsibility of maintaining the schedule for all of the facilities and meeting spaces in the church. St. Joe's had over fifty active ministries in the parish, and at least half to three-quarters of them needed regular meeting space or facilities for weekly meetings or larger events.

I loved my job! Working for the Church was a far cry from the secular and corporate world, thank Goodness! Lou and Fr. Louis became more like father figures than bosses, and Donna and I and the other eight or ten other "workers in the vineyard" found more value in our relationships than pushing papers, though the work always got done. We had fun! We laughed, we danced, we party-bombed each other's desks for birthdays, and we found every excuse imaginable to share in libations to celebrate anything that we found worthy of celebration! We lived the joy of our faith and the true meaning of community and we accepted God's abundant gifts for working for the good of His Church.

When Donna moved out of state in 2008, I became responsible for membership and sacraments. Another secretary who managed and edited the parish bulletin from week to week also left around that time, so I acquired that responsibility too. The major projects drew to a close, I handed off the facility scheduling to my new partner, and

I focused on hospitality, which I still do to this day. Now I welcome new families, give them tours of the building (like Fr. John had done for me), I exchange lollipops for hugs from the little ones who visit while their moms come for WINGS or other ministry meetings, and I walk grieving, fearful or tearful visitors down the hall to Jesus in the Tabernacle, or to the same crucifix I knelt under when I was first diagnosed with cancer.

The parish office is home to me—still now, after ten years. It's where I worship, where I work, where I celebrate with my friends, and where I am privileged to introduce strangers to Jesus. That's the fire that fuels me to this day—bringing people to Jesus. After six years of being on the RCIA team, I decided to leave the team and broaden my audience to the whole parish. Now in the weekly bulletin I channel all the heart, knowledge and energy I have for teaching the Faith into lessons that can be read by over a thousand people each week. Fr. Louis has grown to trust me and he gives me free reign to put in the bulletin anything I want, so I pour out week after week every spiritual lesson I have learned since my faith journey began. He also commissioned me to participate in a "vision committee" for the parish through which I have developed two annual workshops for the parish on evangelization. I still love to teach. I still grow in my fervor to bring people to Jesus and to share with them God's endless forgiveness, mercy and love. And I still love my job!

For the past couple years, God has been teaching me all about that forgiveness, mercy and love and has been all about the business of healing the wounds of my heart. The proof of this has been endless. He has blessed and entrusted me now with seven godchildren to love, teach, worry about and pray for. He's provided me with spiritual directors to help me continue to grow and learn and purge and heal. He's removed many obstacles to my practice of virtue (by that I mean He removed from my daily life many people that tempted me to be less than what God wants me to be), and he continues to give me new life, new hope, and new inspiration to keep moving forward.

Just this week, as I was writing this final chapter, I received a Facebook "friend request". It was Carolyn. She said she was happy to finally find me and that she thought of me often over the years. Just seeing her face, looking at her pictures and reading her Facebook posts made me realize for the first time that we are far different people than we were in college. I certainly changed—I don't know why I never considered the idea that she would too. People move on from friendships all the time, but for some reason that one was different for me. I couldn't let it go. I suppose it had something to do with my temperament (which I'll explain in a moment) and never having closure or anyone else to fill the void that she had left in my life. For whatever reason, that wound became part of me and I just accepted that I would be nursing it for the rest of my life.

But God doesn't want our wounds to go unhealed. In a single moment—a moment that was totally unsolicited and unexpected—I was healed. In that instant when I realized how different we are now, I felt like the hemorrhaging woman who touched the cloak of Jesus and was instantly healed. The bleeding stopped and I was set free.

On another note, in February 2014 George took me on the most perfectly exotic and romantic honeymoon-re-do trip of a lifetime to Maui, Hawaii for a week. We spent the entire week whale-watching (from the water and from shore), shopping for souvenirs, laying on the beach, hiking Haleakala, taking the four-hour waterfall-speckled Road to Hana, snorkeling, taking a sunset dinner cruise, and capturing the most unbelievably "ideal" and picturesque memories on camera that I could've ever imagined. And we had romance. Lots and lots of romance! It was absolutely perfect in every way and well worth the sixteen years we had to wait to experience it!

After Maui, the healing continued. I was introduced to a book called *The Temperament God Gave You* by Art & Laraine Bennett. That, and a second book that Fr. Louis recommended to me, *The Enneagram: A Christian Perspective* by Richard Rohr & Andreas Ebert taught me the single-most validating and wound-healing lesson of my life thus far. That lesson is that God not only created me with a hole in my heart that only He can fill, but that He also purposely created me in a way that is fundamentally different than the way he created others. *I view and respond to the world around me differently than others do.*

I thought I knew myself well, as I imagine everybody does. I am the only one who plays an active role in each and every one of my memories, and I am the only one who hears every thought that passes through my mind. I'm the only one who knows all of my secrets, fears and dreams (except for God, of course), and I'm the only one who cares how right I am about my own opinions and beliefs. Who could know me better than I know myself? Turns out, I learned, that even though I may have known myself better than anyone else, I didn't know myself quite as well as I thought I did.

I thought everything was a matter of being right or wrong. (I, of course, always believing myself to be on the side of "right"!) But God created us all to experience the world in *different* ways—all right and true and good in their own ways, but still subject to the same truth and will of God. I understand that God created each of us, individually, in His own image and likeness, but still it surprises me that the people I have spent a lifetime with can still view the world so differently than I do!

These fundamental life-reacting differences have been defined for thousands of years in different personality and temperament models. They all agree that to some extent, parts of our personalities, and the ways in which we see and react to the world around us, are hard-wired into our souls and will never change. With much time, prayer and practice, we hope to reach a level of maturity, wisdom, understanding and grace to dig deeper than our knee-jerk, gut reactions, to respond to the world around us with Christ-like charity and humility, but our first interior responses will always be the same.

For me, those interior responses come from what they call a "melancholic" temperament, or what the Enneagram calls a "Type One". When I read in each book the descriptions of this temperament, my life changed. For the first time since college with Carolyn, I felt validated, understood, and to some extent excused for being all that I am (and all that I am not).

Suddenly, I began to recognize how my temperament influenced nearly every thought, decision and reaction I had, and for the first time in my life, knowing that God created me with a melancholic life view for some great and masterful purpose beyond my understanding, I had peace. I realized all the self doubt, all the seemingly unforgiveable guilt I felt for seeing things differently than other people did, and for struggling so desperately to relate to people, was simply, yet again, Satan's twist on God's perfect truth. God delights in our differences! He delights in *everything* He's created!

I am an "idealist". I have high ideals and expectations of myself and others, and I am critical (of myself and others) when those ideals are not met. I am scrupulous and constantly concerned about doing things "right". I am more concerned about principles than I am about people's feelings. I am introverted and introspective. Surprise, surprise, I get my energy and peace from being alone, as opposed to being with other people. I am "slow to process stimuli" but my reaction is intense and it lasts a very long time. (Case and point: Carolyn!) I am spiritual and reflective and I am quite organized and attentive to detail. I am a good teacher and am enthusiastic about spurring others on to work and mature and grow. (Though this is a blessing in the classroom or in editing the bulletin, it is more often perceived as being "on my high horse", which can easily rub people the wrong way.) The inner child in me will always be desperate to earn the love of my parents, bosses, God and George by meeting their expectations, and I am devastated when I fall short of pleasing them.

The Enneagram describes a "Type One" this way (paraphrased): "When they see something that approximately matches their ideal of perfection, they are beside themselves with joy, but as soon as someone or something falls short of their ideal, they are greatly disappointed." In that description lies the healing of my deep-seeded wound of infertility. Though I still want babies and hurt and cry and question God's purpose for my life sometimes, I finally understand that God has not rejected me. Instead, I am disappointed that my ideals have not been met. More than wanting to be a mom, I wanted to be the "ideal woman". In my mind, that ideal was personified by my Mom—a devoted wife, a stay-at-home mother of four, and a homemaker. That was God's ideal for *her*. His ideal for me is apparently somewhat different. Somehow that takes away the sting of disappointment. Somehow that gives me hope that meeting God's expectations is still possible—and that inspires me all day every day to discern and conform to His will.

Knowing these things about myself, I cannot stress enough, has brought me more peace than any other lesson I have ever learned. When I feel myself getting angry, irritated or emotional (which, though comes on slowly, can easily become overwhelming for me and the people around me), I can recognize now that it's not me *personally* that is in conflict with (or being rejected by) other people. It is my set of *ideals* that is being challenged, which in many cases is being called into question not by that person, *personally*, but by the Holy Spirit, which always causes me to sit up and take notice.

I'm learning that perfection is in the *practice* of the Faith. It's in having and showing mercy, as God so perfectly bestows on me mercy. Being pleasing to God does not mean that I have to be a cloistered nun. He created each of us individually and He leads each of us to perfection by way of our own path—all through Him, with Him and in Him, but in our own way and in our own time. He put us in this world to love it, and the people in it, just as they are—just as He loves us as we are.

I've come to realize God lovingly fashioned me to be just who I am, what I am, and where I am. And He, the great Author of Life, introduced me as a character in His-Story in this particular time and place on purpose and for His specific and particular reasons. I figure that must mean He intends to use this world around me, as I know it, to speak to me, to teach me, to inspire me and to lead me home to Him in heaven.

He uses all things to speak to me and to give me love. That means finding pleasure in watching a reality TV show about finding love isn't necessarily a bad thing. And watching secular (non-spiritual) movies and listening to secular music isn't necessarily a bad thing either. For that matter, even finding pleasure itself doesn't mean I've strayed far from God! Not if I recognize Him as the Giver of that gift, and recognize the message of love He sends me through it.

I now try to find God in all things. Secular songs like "I Wanta Know What Love Is" and "Everything I Do I Do It For You" have become prayers and love songs between me and Jesus. As "The Bachelor" or "The Bachelorette" offers roses to those they want to know better, God puts roses in my path and beckons me to stay with Him a while longer, to get to know Him better, to find love and security in His new and exciting embrace. Scenes like one in the movie "Signs" about an alien invasion of Earth where Mel Gibson holds his asthmatic son saying, "Breathe with me…the air is coming…we are the same…" becomes the verse that lulls me to sleep at night when I can't settle the thoughts in my mind and I imagine my head resting on the chest of Jesus. Yes! God created all things and in all things He can speak to me and love me—and I, Him! I feel like the dad in "My Big Fat Greek Wedding" who can prove every word comes from a root word in Greek—give me a secular song, TV show or movie, and I'll show you that it comes from God!

How exciting life has become since that revelation! How enjoyable and interesting and challenging my days have become since I started looking for Him in all things! And in all people, too. That's a bit more challenging for me, to find His image and likeness in those who constantly cry "woe-is-me", or the people who think they're better than everyone else or exempt from the rules, and especially in those who dare to say I do not do my job well! But He's there too—in them—in all of them. And He even uses them to speak to me and love me when I open myself to hear and to be loved.

That's it. That's the difference between "Me Then" and "Me Now". I've gotten to know God, and by knowing Him, I've grown to trust Him, and through that trust, I learned to love Him, and be loved by Him. Just like George's and my love story, how it began. First we met. Then we asked questions about each other and discerned the similarities in what we valued and in what we enjoyed. We opened ourselves to love. We spent time together and shared our deepest fears and loftiest dreams. We wrote love letters and looked often at pictures of each other. We made each other laugh and we made each other cry. We easily overlooked each other's shortcomings because they easily dissolved in the ocean of all that we found good in each other.

It's the same with God. All you have to do is meet Him, talk to Him, spend time with Him, laugh with Him, cry with Him, and look often at pictures of Him. Invite Him to go where you go and He will eagerly accompany you. He longs deeply for you to know Him the way he knows you—intimately, individually, honestly, and completely.

I know this is not the end of my story. I know God is continuing to heal the wounds of my heart and to reveal Himself to me. I know I have a long way to go to get to Heaven, but I have peace. I am energized by my search for truth. God continues to give me strength to persevere. I am evermore willing to surrender to the will of God, and to trust Him with all that I am.

I hope you are not disappointed by my lack of a "happy ending" here—no climax, like my being able to tell you George and I now have babies. We do not. Nor do I have a definitive answer to all of life's confusion, pain, suffering and disappointments. But I do have peace. I do have hope. I do have my George. We do have a God who loves us. And I do mean it every time I make the Sign of the Cross and say: "Jesus, I belong to You; Jesus, I surrender to You; Jesus, I trust in You."